EAST END TO EAST COAST

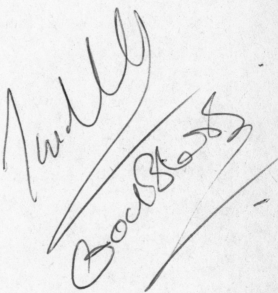

EAST END
TO
EAST COAST

Martin Saunders

AUTHENTIC PUBLISHING
Milton Keynes, England

EAST END TO EAST COAST
Copyright © 2002 Martin Saunders

First published 2002 by Authentic Publishing,
9 Holdom Avenue, Bletchley, Milton Keynes, Bucks,
MK1 1QR, UK

British Library Cataloguing in Publication Data

A catalogue record for this book is available from the
British Library

1-86024-276-6

Cover design by David Lund
Printed in Great Britain by Biddles Ltd., Suffolk,

For Joanna

CONTENTS

ACKNOWLEDGEMENTS

With thanks to Julia Swindells, David Whitley, Jim de Rennes, Jason Lewis, Hilary Robertson, Maria James, Julia Fisher, John Self, Phil and Sarah Warburton, Dave Gatward, Dan Rookwood, Phil Thain, Stanley Pea, Ian Bunning, Adam Aspinall, Mr Tony Wilson, everyone at Crossroads and Christ's Tabernacles, Malcolm Down, David Lund, Liz Williams, Sgt Val Suarez, Pedro Gonzales, Terry and Christine Miller, David, Michael, Rio etc, my whole family and Westbury Wanderers FC.

With extremely special thanks to all of Tough Talk and their families, without whose help, hospitality and 'hardness' this book would not have been possible.

FOREWORD

Martin Saunders virtually lived with us for six weeks, sharing, during that time, the highs and lows of Tough Talk. He always promised to give an honest and unbiased report, as he wrote the story of *East End to East Coast*. This he has achieved with great sense of humour and with his own, unique view of things: capturing the atmosphere and excitement of our meetings, together with the values of Tough Talk. He insightfully reveals the real characters behind the hard images, and uses engaging storytelling and vibrant metaphor to bring them alive on the page..

In *East End to East Coast* Martin will take you on a journey through the strange world of innovative evangelists, Tough Talk. It has been said that they are the most extraordinary in the country and I am proud to be associated with them.

Martin had me laughing and crying at the same moment, and I would warmly recommend this as a great book that, hopefully, will inspire you.

Ian McDowall, Tough Talk

Chapter 1

East End

When you're cruising in a plane at ten thousand feet, the people on the ground look very, very small. But when you're standing on the ground looking up at the sky, that same plane looks no more than a needle, threading the clouds above. It's all about perspective.

A giant flying bullet called Boeing pierces the evening sky over the Home Counties, and I'm inside. Had I been on the ground at this moment, perhaps lying on some Surrey lawn with a glass in one hand and a broadsheet newspaper in the other, this great metal gravity-betrayer would have meant very little to me. The ants inside it, busy with all the details of fetching and carrying that their lives contain, would have meant even less. But I'm not on the ground, sipping Pimms and reading *The Times*. I'm on Virgin Atlantic Flight V101 from Heathrow, juggling three cartons of Ribena and folding away my complimentary copy of *The Sun*. So, for the next eight hours, I'm vacuum-packed into this tin with 200 other souls. And suddenly the ants have got a lot bigger. That's where perspective comes in.

Before we go any further, I'm not important in this story. My name's on the cover, but there's little more you'll need to know if I'm honest. I'm a journalist by trade, or at least I like to think I am, and I'm fortunate enough to have stumbled upon a bona fide story right now. Or a bunch of crackpots – although I'm hoping for the sake of everyone's reputation that it's the former.

Anyway, perspective. It's about what you see, and what you don't. When you meet someone new, you find out about their life, and then you *know* about them. It doesn't mean that their life changes; it doesn't mean that they start or stop doing what they do. They've always done it; just out of your field of vision. And when you find out about it, they just keep on going – keep on doing what they've always done – and their life doesn't change one bit. But if you meet the right new people, and get a clear enough perspective, it might just change *your* life.

My perspective right now is allowing me to take in a group of men: a group of very big, very British men. If I'd never met them, they'd still be taking this very same flight, sitting in the very same seats. I wouldn't be here though. I'd be on the lawn, drinking Pimms and reading *The Times*. And Tough Talk would just be a troop of flying ants, sailing silently overhead. At this moment though, I'm pretty pleased about my perspective.

Suddenly, the plane lurches sideways, then tilts as if King Kong has just aimed a right hook at its defenceless wing. Lights flash, hostesses panic, children scream. That Hollywood moment with the falling oxygen masks plays right before my eyes in 3-D, Widescreen and Glorious Technicolor. My stomach is doing somersaults . . . looks like a couple of the engines are too. This really doesn't look too good. *I think we're going to crash.*

No, wait. If you really want perspective, You have to begin at the beginning. Let's go back a few months.

* * *

It seems ironic that at the exact moment that Tough Talk first wandered into my life, I happened to be sweating it out in a gym. I've never been the most athletic, muscular or fit member of the community, and my sporadic efforts at regular exercise have always just been a vague and futile attempt at getting a brief clutch at 'good health' before young-age spread has really started to kick in. Still, I decided to join a gym after leaving University, partly because of girlfriend pressure and partly because I was fed up with looking like a greedy hamburger salesman.

My choice of gymnasium involved a lot of psychology. Had I signed up at the local YMCA, with its low, low prices and collection of scary-looking medieval torture equipment, I'd probably have never gone back after the first week. Alternatively, if I'd plumped for one of those real, serious gyms, with a membership consisting of several champion weightlifters and half the cast of *Gladiators*, and with a reputation for its impressive Mafia links, I'd almost certainly have been scared off halfway through the induction. This left only one choice open to me.

Thus the first I ever heard of Tough Talk was through one of six giant plasma television screens which lined the walls of the impressively furnished health club which had just emptied my bank account. Unfortunately, I had realised that the combination of guilt and money was going to be the only sure-fire recipe to ensure that I'd keep going back. At the price I would be paying every month, I'd simply have to force myself to go every other day in order to somehow turn it into money well spent. Madness I know. Yet without this piece of flawed reasoning, it's very likely indeed that a few months later, I wouldn't have been getting on no plane, crazy fool.

At the crucial moment, I was performing a series of barely-controlled lurches on a machine that had promised to give me 'the ultimate full body workout.' Arms, legs, pushes and pulls were all combining to cause me the maximum amount of pain, and I was in dire need of a distraction. For a few moments I submerged myself in the seedy and voyeuristic world of people-watching, as my cruel eyes divined the fit from the fat, the dedicated from the once-a-monthers, and those who gently perspire from those who look like they've just returned from a visit to Niagara Falls. This gave me only a couple of minutes' comfort though – there's only so much pleasure to be derived from looking at the sweaty backs of your fellow sufferers – and I realised that it was time to resort to the lowest common denominator and watch TV. Three channel choices presented themselves on my side of the gym. First, MTV were presenting a rundown of the Euro-Pop chart (incidentally, the most nauseating music scene to be found anywhere in the world). Second, Eurosport had live coverage of the world tractor-pulling championships from Hamburg (tempting, but I decided against it). Which only left the local BBC news, which seemed to be running some kind of dull human-interest story. I briefly considered a return to voyeurism, but the burning in my thigh muscles screamed for an entertaining diversion. Grudgingly, I gave the cat-up-a-tree report a chance.

Except it wasn't a cat-up-a-tree story. It was a rather bizarre tale of unlicensed boxing matches in the churches of East London. Apparently, this guy was putting up boxing rings in front of altars, and getting large crowds in to watch two blokes belt each other's brains out in the name of the Lord. This man had, by all accounts, been a nasty piece of work in his former life, until one day God appeared to him in a cloud of holy smoke and he saw the light. Redeemed, he then decided that he needed to spread the word amongst all his friends and associates, but was faced with the problem that most of them were either boxers, bodybuilders or hardmen. He'd have enough trouble getting them out of a gym, let alone coercing them into the dusty pews of a church (precisely the reverse of my own problem). Hence his novel idea. He realised that the only way to get his friends to cross the giant divide between these two worlds would be to combine them both in one place. So he did: he placed a boxing ring in a church, put on bouts between up-and-coming fighters, and then tagged a Christian message onto the end.

If nothing else, it was a great story. The BBC certainly thought so, and from the lack of pain emanating from my lower body, I deduced that my thighs agreed. I quickly made a mental note of all this after it dawned on me that it'd be very useful in the morning. You see, when I'm not in this torture chamber, I spend my time as a journalist for London's Premier Radio – a religious broadcaster which thrives on this sort of thing. I could picture our features editor right now, slapping me on the back and pinning a gold star to my lapel for good story-spotting. Maybe we could get this fellow into the studio, I thought, and get him to beat up a couple of the presenters live on air.

But wait – my eyes flicked back to Auntie Beeb – there was more to the story. It seemed that on the night that this feast of sport and spirituality was filmed, he wasn't working alone, but was being assisted by three friends with equally seedy backgrounds: Arthur White, Steve Johnson and Ian McDowall. Three bad men from the wrong side of town who, like their pugilist-promoting friend, had done a lot of bad things before hitting the 'road to Damascus'. It was all beginning to sound like the pitch for a Hollywood blockbuster, so it seemed fitting when the amused television cameraman panned across to a publicity poster that displayed the Scorcese-spoofing legend 'Godfellas.' Below the lettering, Arthur, Steve and Ian appeared wearing sharp suits and sharper expressions. It seemed that they'd been called in to add some extra muscle to an evening that was already brimming with testosterone, and to deliver the hard-hitting Christian message at the end. This was all very interesting – my mental notepad was filling up fast. I decided it would be a good idea to get off the torture machine now and transfer all these names, ages and bicep measurements to paper. Yet, as I looked away at last from the television screen, I realised that there'd be no need for the usual 'two-minute cool-down'. I'd been caught in the Tough Talk tractor-beam for the first time – my exercises must have ground to a halt five minutes earlier.

* * *

I'm still waiting for the turning point in my life, when a mid-life crisis or a brush with death turns me into a morning person. As it is, I'm about as much use before nine a.m. as an umbrella in a nuclear strike. On this particular morning though, the steady pump of adrenaline in my veins was making me feel like I'd stolen a cup of God's coffee, and had persuaded me, for the first time in my life, to take the early train.

I made it to work a full forty-five minutes early, made myself an unnecessary cup of caffeine, and waited impatiently for the arrival of Julia Fisher – Premier Radio's features editor and expert on all things quirky-spiritual. If anyone was going to be interested in my story of boxers, villains and hardmen, it'd be Julia. So, after a quick Internet search had yielded no extra information, and after hearing the lady herself stroll through the office doors, I trotted excitedly round to her desk with notepad in hand and tail wagging.

Within ten seconds my heart had been broken. My opening gambit, which ran along the lines of 'you're not going to believe what's going on in East London', was met with a swift and crushing response.

'Yes, I know. I've interviewed them before. Here's their number.'

This staccato series of statements was almost wholly depressing. It seemed that there'd be no gold star for me now. Yet those final three words, 'Here's their number,' were laced with hope. Perhaps there was still a story here. I thanked Julia and made for my desk.

One conversation with the gruff-voiced Arthur White later, I was confused. In the news report that I'd seen, Arthur's 'Godfellas' had been providing the knockout punch at the end of the promoter's altar-side boxing match. Naturally, I had assumed that the two were strongly linked, but this wasn't the case. Arthur explained that he worked as part of a group of London-based men who travelled the country spreading the Christian message, and that his appearance as a 'Godfella' was just one snapshot of his daily work. Much to the disappointment of the marketing man within me, the 'Godfellas' didn't actually exist – not by that name anyway.

'We're a registered charity called Tough Talk,' he explained. 'We spread the message of the gospel through telling the stories of how our lives have been changed. And through the lifting of weights.'

'Weights?' I exclaimed, with one hand clasped to my spinning head. 'I thought you were boxers.'

'Powerlifters. We put on a demonstration of powerlifting.'

'Are you any good?'

'Well, I've been World Champion twice. Does that count?'

Powerlifting, for the uninitiated, is very similar to classic weightlifting, but with a bit more back-breaking, shoulder-splitting, arm-bursting force shoved into it. There are three main disciplines – so pay attention. First, there's lying flat on a thin table, pushing a heavily loaded bar up and down at your shoulders, which is called a 'bench-press'. This is completely impossible, and anyone who tells you that they can do it is lying. Second, there's the 'squat', where a competitor rests a ridiculously danger-ous amount of weight on his shoulders, whilst standing bent at the knees. Most people who do too much of this end up a few inches shorter than when they began, which is possibly where the name comes from. Finally, lifting copious amounts of weight from the ground with a straight back, shouting a bit and then dropping it all, is called a 'deadlift'. A few weeks before our conversation, Arthur had won a World Championship gold in this dis-cipline. So, if nothing else, he's good to have around when you need to move the refrigerator.

'Powerlifting,' I repeated. 'I'm afraid I'm not familiar with that.'

As Arthur explained the ins and outs of his sport, Julia Fisher appeared in the doorway of my office, waving something rectangular. Taking several confident strides toward me, she thrust a small blood-red book into my hand and whispered 'thought this might be useful.' I looked down to discover that the legend 'Tough Talk' was emblazoned on the front cover, next to three terrify-ing mugshots. One of the three, I quickly deduced, was Arthur. Goodness, aren't you pretty, I thought.

'So do you want to come down and meet us?' he asked suddenly.

I gazed down again at the nightclub-bouncer head in front of me, and gulped.

'You could come down next Wednesday,' he continued without prompting. 'We're doing a presentation in one of the biggest schools in this part of London.'

It sounded like a good story. But it would involve going into a hard-as-nails East London school and interviewing big scary men. I do have a newshound within me, but unfortunately it's Scooby Doo.

'Well,' he asked impatiently, 'would you like to come along?'

* * *

I stood and waited for Arthur in the car park of Loughton station, as the rays of a CFC-fuelled British winter gently warmed me. I'd decided that I would take up Arthur's offer and 'come along' to interview him at his home and then watch Tough Talk's in-school power-lifting demonstration. My companion (a man who is affectionately known to friends as 'Little Phil') and I hardly cast giant shadows on the East End tarmac and as we waited to finally meet this ogre – who until now had been no more real than his menacing photograph – we allowed ourselves a humorous exchange on what to expect.

'Do you think he'll drive a Land Rover?' I asked.

'No' replied Phil with a smile. 'He probably squeezes himself into a Mini.'

As we chuckled at the thought of this man, a World Champion at being really big, somehow threading his gargantuan frame through the needle-eye of the most impractical vehicle known to man, the truth arrived like a triple dose of Alka-Seltzer.

'Guess I was closer,' I spluttered.

The door of Arthur White's motor caravan swung open, and a voice straight out of the Queen Vic beckoned us forwards. The figure inside was trying very hard to smile, but years of looking hard for a living were making it difficult. My first impression, thanks largely to the facial hair, was 'Mammoth.'

'I'm Arthur,' said the Mammoth.

'You don't say . . . ' was replaced just in time by a pleasant reciprocal introduction.

Phil had legged it already. He'd brought his own car (presumably he felt that this would be safer), and was getting ready to follow us. So now it was just me, the Mammoth, and a small house on wheels.

I managed to drag myself on board, ask Arthur how he was, and talk nervously for a few moments about the merits of the Central Line. After this rather poor use of oxygen had helped me to fill at least thirty seconds, and appropriated at least a couple of nods from the Mammoth, we fell into silence. It wasn't an unpleasant silence – certainly as far as he was concerned – and it allowed me a few moments to fully take in the man next to me.

Being a boy from South London, where newsagents don't devote whole shelves to Spanish villa brochures, and where every vacant shop isn't plastered with adverts for some illiterate gangland criminal's first book, I'm not used to people like this. Arthur looks like he's been in a battle – not a fight, a battle – and although his spirit betrays a youthful vibrancy once you get to know him, it's clear from the start that the body is hardened. You get the feeling that if you stood Arthur, tree-like, in the middle of a monsoon, his trunk would stand up to the weathering. Actually, a tree provides a better illustration than an extinct marauding beast, for Arthur is indeed a man capable of bearing great weights on his shoulders. Add to that the planed and chiselled nature of his dignified features; the trimmed perfection of his well-groomed beard; the aged wisdom of his knowing eyes, and the resemblance becomes just about complete.

'We're here,' barked the Tree.

And we were, but the house that we'd parked outside didn't look big enough for a man with his shoulders.

Arthur gave me a cup of tea, and sat me on a sprawling sofa. I turned on my tape recorder, and he told me his story.

For a lengthy period in his life, powerlifting was Arthur White's god. He first trained at fourteen, started to compete in his early twenties, and shortly after that found himself representing Great Britain. By the age of twenty-five, he'd established himself as one of the rising stars of the sport. After a while, he found himself tasting a little success, and quickly began to grow fond of the flavour. It was at this point that he discovered that a good diet and plenty of visits to the gym weren't the only secret recipes. There was a quicker route to goal. Steroids.

What his fellow musclemen failed to explain, in their casual locker room advice, was that often steroids are only the first stop on a long-distance train. So after the sport gently led Arthur to performance-enhancing drugs, the drugs grabbed him by the throat and took him to meet their friends. First up, he came face to face with Little Miss Amphetamines, who was great for a few flirtatious encounters – a laugh and a joke – but in the end failed to satisfy. Then she too pushed Arthur on to meet another friend; another foe; another turn of the screw.

'So for somewhere between eight and ten years I had a steroid and cocaine addiction which basically destroyed my life' Arthur explained, in well-rehearsed and oft-trod words from which he still couldn't detach his emotions.

I really wanted to say something intelligent then: something that would show him how totally down-with-it and streetwise I was. I wanted to look surprised but not shocked; involved but unfazed. So, taking a deep breath, I searched within my soul for the right words with which to respond to his revelation. In the library in my head I looked at empathy, flicked through maturity and read every page of cool, calm and collected. Then, after careful thought, I prepared to make the incredible sound.

'That sounds bad,' I said, with all the stupidity a boy could muster. Bad. *Bad*? I'm going around calling myself a writer and the most intelligent word I can pluck from my supposedly vast vocabulary to describe a ten-year battle with hard drugs is one I learned when I was two years old.

'It was *bad*,' said Arthur, adding emphasis to show his disappointment at my trivialising tone. 'It was very bad. Nine years ago, I was literally killing myself with the drug addiction. The drugs made my heart expand – my heart ballooned to the size of a small football and it was going to explode. Seven of my good friends, including one man who was the 'World's Strongest Man' three times, all died of their various addictions. So the drugs were actually killing me. I was a walking time bomb.'

Curiosity jumped up out of my throat with the most obvious of questions.

'Then what happened, nine years ago?'

He looked up suddenly, as if I'd knocked his brain off-balance.

'You don't know the half of it yet,' he half whispered.

* * *

Now I have no idea who you might be, reading this. You may be of a churchgoing persuasion, but then again, you may not. So for the sake of the latter group, who statistically dominate the reading public, a few words of warning. In a moment, we're going to hit the J-word for the first time in open play. We've already had 'Christian' a couple of times. We've had several mentions of 'God' and you're still with us. But the J-word is a totally different matter altogether. The J-word is used to spit and curse. The J-word is found on the walls of infant classrooms and it takes half as long to grow out of it. The J-word rhymes with school cabbage, or mad people on street corners, or old women on hard dusty pews. The J-word means bad hair, bad clothes, bad breath. It means hollow, empty, irrelevant. It means man-made. It means crutch.

That's what the J-word means on planet Earth today. Please attach your own definition if none of the above suffice. It's on its way in the next couple of pages. You have been warned. Please don't leave us.

* * *

I drained the dainty china coffee-cup as Arthur fiddled in cupboards, bags and boxes. He stopped talking to me briefly so that he could replenish the biscuits that had magically vanished. Glancing down at his table I caught a glimpse of the brash red corner of *Time* magazine. *Time* magazine? This oaf read *Time* magazine? How could he know anything about world affairs, business and economics, fine art and opera? How could he even understand the reader's letters? How could he even understand the pictures? He talks in a common accent, for heaven's sake. It must belong to his wife. Yes, his wife. How could I find out about his wife?

'My wife,' announced Arthur, reading my mind, making me cough and terrifying me, 'is an incredible woman. I love her very much indeed.'

I could sense from the scurrying sounds of the pensive little creature squirming in his throat as he spoke that we were ready for part two now.

'My wife and I split up. I had been having an adulterous affair with another woman, and over a period of about four years I returned and left seven times.'

Seven times. The number rolled around my head as I tried not to flinch or scowl. *Seven*. This lady is either mad or stupid, and probably a mix of the two, I'm thinking. I mean, you just don't hear about that do you? People leave each other every day of the week; the divorce statistics will spell that out for you. Occasionally they come crawling back together too, and often they even split up again once a smell or a fight or a memory reminds them why they did it the first time. But seven times? . . . Arthur looked at me, read my mind again, huffed, and then continued.

'I know what you're thinking. But when I left for the seventh time, she turned her back and said 'no more.' Which was quite right and normal. I'm surprised she didn't do it earlier than that. You're probably thinking she was mad for not saying that after the first time I left. But she kept taking me back, kept believing that things would change and get better. Until that last time. Then she said that I had to see a counsellor to sort me out.'

'What did you do?'

'I wanted my wife back. I wanted my family back. And I really did, this time. So I went to see this bloke that she recommended. Now it just so happened that this counsellor was also a Christian. That didn't interest me too much – I didn't think much of Christians. I thought then that all Christian men were wimps. But I knew I wanted to get off of the drugs and back with my wife. So I went to see him, and after about an hour he told me I had to go away and choose. Now we have choices to make every day, and I'd made some particularly bad choices at that time. I had to choose between my wife and another woman, between the family I once had and starting another family. I had to choose between the life I was living, and the life I once had.

'Now I thought long and hard about this. I tossed and turned about it. Because the life I'd left behind had been a good life, with a happy marriage, successful business, and successful sports career. By comparison, I was living a pretty evil life at this time: living in the East End of London, in a cramped and squalid bedsit, running an illegal debt collection business, with a life that revolved around violence and drugs. And you'd think it would make it so easy, when you think about it like that and lay it all out there in front of your eyes. But it's still hard to think straight when your life is such a mess.'

I decided it was time to ask the question again. You remember – that blindingly obvious one from earlier. I'd been keeping it in my top pocket.

'So what happened? What happened nine years ago that got you off the drugs and put you back in this family home?'

Arthur straightened up, stared at me and smiled. Then he looked across to Little Phil, my unusually silent friend, and smiled at him too.

'I met someone. At 3.30 in the morning, in a freezing cold car park in the East End of London. I met Him in the car park of Spitalfields market. I stretched out my arms, I screamed out for help, and I met . . . '

Hold it. I still don't think we're ready for this. As I said, I don't know who you are of course. You might be a Methodist minister, have a degree in theology, or you might be a car park attendant from Spitalfields market. You could be a Christian, you could be an atheist, you could be anything in between or sideways or beyond. But whoever and whatever you are, it's a fair bet that the J-word is a little bit uncomfortable for you. The Sunday school teacher gets upset when his children shout it in the street as a swear word. The car park attendant gets upset by it when it forms the basis of an embarrassingly unfunny bumper sticker. The Christian gets coy about it. The atheist tries to pretend it doesn't exist. And everyone else in between attaches their own meaning and conjures up their own picture for it, as long as they fly nicely wide of the mark and it doesn't challenge or offend them too much.

Perhaps that's because the J-word has always suffered from that kind of reaction. The man whom the J-word belonged to was a revolutionary, after all. Nobody could really cope with or understand Him at the time. But some people believed that His name wasn't a swear word, that He was nothing to be embarrassed or coy about, that the claims He made about Himself were true and He had the scars to prove it.

Today, some people still believe that He really, really did exist, that His life changed the world and that, far from being irrelevant, His life is still of ultimate importance to everyone. That's what some people believe. That's what Arthur White believes. And in this story, when we use the J-word, it refers to the most important figure in world history, not a little man in a beard and sandals.

Right, now we're ready.

'Jesus.'

Chapter 2

Inside the Soviet Military Base

The world loves a big strong man. How else would Arnold Schwarzenegger have become one of the highest paid actors of all time? Why otherwise would the World Wrestling Federation sell tickets, T-shirts and action figures in such massive quantities? Our billboards, magazines, TV screens and beaches don't lie – everyone likes a good set of muscles. There's something about that ripple of biceps, triceps, abs and pecs under tight skin, like polished rocks packed in fleshy plastic, that makes women go weak at the knees and men go green with envy. And sometimes vice versa. Muscles are something for men to aspire to, and when we've grown ourselves some, after hours of pain and perseverance, we fail to be satisfied. Because once we have grown our happy little muscles, we meet someone else with bigger ones and instantly feel small again. So we step back on to the leg-rack, or the back-crush or the arm-break, and repeat our repetitions to infinity. That's why gyms are bad for your health: the giant in the corner, lifting a ton without even breaking sweat, will always have bigger arms than you, will always be able to lift more, will always look better in a tight pink vest. That colossus – who incidentally only wears the pink vest because he can, and because no one will mention or even look at it – he'll give you an exercising disorder, he will.

The world doesn't love a Christian. If we did, famous Christians wouldn't spend half their time pretending that they weren't. Christianity is all about idolising the unseen, worshipping a force far bigger and greater than our own, and making that force more important than us. In this age of celebrity – of staged fights, staged hair and staged love lives – it's not hard to see why that kind of worldview just doesn't fit in. We don't want anything bigger than ourselves. We want stars: pop stars, movie stars, sports stars and TV stars. And then we can lift them up to a comfortable height, and worship them. After all, we all need something to worship, to follow, to believe in. But while these flash-in-the-pan legends and luminaries prance naively on their paper pedestal, they don't know what we know. We know that we've only lifted them *so* high, and that when the time is right, we can drag them right back down again, purely for our entertainment and shameless *schadenfreude*. And then we know – because Andy Warhol told us – that when the time is right, someone will give us a hand up onto that pedestal, and everyone will be screaming our names. We don't need God. We've got Arnold Schwarzenegger.

* * *

Three weeks after my visit to Arthur's, I found myself sitting in a local, very South London pub with a good friend of mine. He'd decided that this would be a good opportunity to tell me about his troubles: job trouble, woman trouble and car trouble. All in all, it sounded like my friend was in trouble. I'm not very good at answers, so I just kept listening to the problems. And there sure were a lot of them. Did I mention family trouble, or illness trouble? No? He did. He mentioned them all, and I kept on listening.

'What I need mate,' he droned as I drank deeply from the only possible escape route, 'is a nice girlfriend.'

I nodded and made a sound which was supposed to sound sympathetic, but due to the bubbles in my nose sounded like a mocking snigger. He continued unperturbed.

'I need a woman who I can take out with the lads, who's nice looking, who doesn't want to get too serious, who's great in the sack, and who's not been with too many blokes before. Actually, no, I want her to be a virgin.'

'A virgin?'

'With big breasts.'

'You want an experienced virgin . . . '

'Yes.' He failed to spot the oxymoron.

'Who is nice looking, and who you can take out with the lads . . . '

'But who the other lads won't try it on with.'

'Right.'

I don't know where he developed his checklist. It's probably got something to do with pornography. It's probably got something to do with television. Come to think of it, that tends to mean the same thing these days. Oh, and just in case you were wondering, this isn't an 'I've got this friend who's got this problem' kind of friend. He's real enough. In fact there are several of him.

My friend seemed to think that his many troubles – and believe me, there were a multitude – would be put to an end if he could just find this one special girl. I couldn't understand that. I mean, would she sort out his boss for him? Would she fix his car? Would she have the magic solution to all his health problems? Probably not. But she would look good on his arm, and give him that tiny but much-sought injection of celebrity, and make him feel warm and special when they got round to faking love.

I worry about my friend. He may have a lot to moan about, and he may moan a lot, but deep down he's a good kid. When I hear him groping around in the dark like this, searching for hope and peace and answers and solutions, it's hard for me to help him find any of them. To me it's clear that he's looking for meaning. He wants something to believe in – a giant coat-hook on which to hang his whole life. The perfect woman might just do that for him, for a while. But then what about afterwards? What about when the passion fades, the personalities begin to grate and the looks begin to go? Where will he hang his coat when it all starts to go wrong?

'I've got a story to tell you,' I said, diving in as he finally took a breath. 'Did I tell you about my afternoon with those powerlifters?'

His expression redefined blankness.

'I went over to East London the other week. Right out towards Essex. Went to chase up a story, about this group of blokes who used to be bouncers, hardmen and gangland nutcases, and now go around evangelising. Really odd story. And when they're evangelising, they lift weights.'

'What, on the streets?'

'No . . .'

'I saw this bloke on the street the other day. French or Belgian I think he was – kept shouting things out of a megaphone, all this doom and gloom stuff about how we're all going to hell unless we repent and become like Him.'

'No, it was in a school,' I protested in vain.

'I mean what kind of advert for religion is that? He's standing there in the middle of a street in a rainbow-striped jumper and a big beard, shouting at people. He's actually wearing those brown sandals, from the stereotype. And people are even taking the long way to their destinations – just so they can avoid him. Two o'clock on a Saturday afternoon in the middle of the high street, and he's standing in twenty square feet of empty pavement.'

'Right, but this was in a school . . . '

'And to cap it all off, he's shouting in broken English through a megaphone that's set to maximum distortion. Even if I did want to listen to him, I'd have only heard the words that he got really excited about. And those tended to be 'burn', 'hell' and 'damnation.' I tell you what – you lot need to get a good PR man in.'

'Us lot?'

'The God squad.'

'But not all Christians are like that. Like I was trying to tell you before – these guys from the East End . . . '

'Hang on a minute mate, I just need to get another beer in if you're going to bore me to death with one of your stories.'

My friend clambered towards the bar, through the packed congregation and heaving pews of this twenty-first century church. Then he raised his hands and gave up an offering to his short-term saviour, an Australian barman. He took the pint, and the crisps, and gave thanks. Then, with much care and thought, he navigated his way back to our corner, dumped the drinks and headed off again, this time to the confessional cubicle.

As I divided the story into manageable bullet-points in my head, I asked myself a question. Why is it that people really don't like talking about matters of eternity? Why is it that whenever the meaning of life crops up in conversation, it's either hastily explained away by a quote from

Douglas Adams, Albert Camus or Monty Python, or else it's immediately given second billing to the big sports story of the day? Surely if there is a God, if there is a deeper meaning to it all, if there is life after death, *if* . . . Well then surely that's the most important thing in the world, isn't it? So why won't we talk about it in our bars, or think about it in our beds? What are we afraid of?

'Big school,' I yelled as my friend returned, anxious to get my mouth open before his. 'East London. 300 kids. Powerlifting demonstration. Children noisy. Nasty life story involving stabbings, fights, guns. Children getting nervous and less noisy. More powerlifting. Another nasty story. Swords. Explanation of how meeting God had saved their lives. Children silent.' And breathe.

He looked at me with big, rattled eyes. Silent, for once, he took a long hard look into his bubbling brown liquid, then gulped at it as he frantically tried to think of something to say. Finally, as denoted by the arrival of a glint in his eye, the well thought-out response jumped into torpedo tube 1.

'You what?' he asked.

'It doesn't matter,' I replied, like a suddenly flat tyre. 'It wasn't a great story anyway.'

Well, actually, that wasn't quite true. It had seemed like a pretty great story to me, as I'd stood and watched it unfold. It's not often that you see something, the like of which you can't recall seeing before. We live in an age of repeats, reissues and cover versions after all. But this, this had literally dripped with originality. When I returned home from my night at the pub, I thought it might be a good idea to check out the Premier Radio website, where I'd published that story about my afternoon in the East End, just to check that I wasn't imagining things. I logged on with slight reluctance – work and play were getting a

little confused here – but soon found the words that confirmed my sanity:

The two hundred and seventy screaming children who had
packed into the high school hall looked barely controllable.
The teachers were having their work cut out trying to keep
them even moderately quiet – it looked as if it was going to
take a miracle to actually silence them. As this mass of 13
and 14 year olds chatted about what they'd had for lunch,
which boy or girl they'd kissed at the weekend, or who they
were going to beat up after school, three men walked onto
the stage.

It became apparent, as these three men introduced themselves, that they were here to talk about God. A number of
derisory moans arose from the cynical audience, many of
whom probably felt about as interested in spirituality as
they did in double mathematics. Yet somehow, by the end of
the hour that followed, nearly three hundred people were
listening intently to the gospel of Jesus Christ. Welcome to
the world of Tough Talk.

The three men at the front are Arthur White, Steve
Johnson and Ian McDowall – the key members of an East
London-based charity which seeks to make the Christian
message real to modern society. Their collective name needs
little explanation once you've seen them – each man is a
giant muscle-bound powerlifter, capable of lifting huge
weights. They wouldn't look out of place on a nightclub
door, or in a gang of hired thugs. But that's hardly surpris-
ing, when they explain that's exactly where they've come
from.

And whilst they're not proud of former lives that included cocaine addictions, knife fighting, violent crime and
life-threatening steroid abuse, the Tough Talk team are
determined to use their stories for good. So, as one member
of the team lifts an increasing amount of weights, another is

sharing personally on a microphone about how meeting Jesus Christ literally saved his life. Then, after a little audience participation, the roles reverse, and another of the team tells his life story whilst more weights are lifted.

These aren't small weights either – at one point Arthur, a former World Powerlifting Champion and current world number 3, lifts an incredible 500 pounds (well over 200 kilos), much to the amazement of the wildly supportive crowd.

By the end of the show, every child is listening intently to Steve's powerful words. His story is breathtaking, and injects a moving degree of humanity and realism into the concept of being a Christian. He used to be a very bad person, but he says that by God's grace he has been saved. It's a message that's not lost even on the cynics. As the team clear their equipment away, many of the audience are lost in thought. This was without question the most dynamic, relevant and effective piece of evangelism that they or I have ever seen.

I had found that experience quite extraordinary, even if my lousy writing skills weren't quite up to conveying the fact. On leaving Arthur's that afternoon, we'd had to rendezvous at the school with Ian and Steve, the other two Tough Talk cornerstones. They were also the proud owners of the other two mugshots on the cover of the book that Julia Fisher had given me. Ian was a shorter, stockier, younger, more sun-tanned version of Arthur; Steve just looked like an extremely nasty football hooligan with a bit of facial scarring. Collectively they looked absolutely terrifying.

Within five minutes I'd realised I had little to fear. None of them can help the way they look – they were built to be mean after all. But inside, beyond those harsh shells, it's obvious that regeneration has taken place. I heard a story once about an abandoned military base in the former Soviet Union that had been taken over by flower people. Bit by bit, they renovated the whole place, planting love where hate used to be – spreading life in a place where death had once been concocted. The two giant cannons which flanked the main gate became flower cranes, hoisting glorious great hanging baskets above the base. Dark, blank prison-like walls were painted with vibrant murals. Military greys and greens were replaced throughout by a rainbow of colours. The whole area took on a new lease of life. That's kind of how it is with Tough Talk, I suppose. Their well-oiled bulks were once designed for harm, once caused little but pain and misery, but then the flower people moved in. Or something like that.

Anyway, we met up in the drama hall of this very large school. A big, angular, modern building with long, endless corridors, it apparently played 'zoo' to nearly three thousand animals, ranging from small mammals to jungle beasts. It seemed likely that visiting speakers would usually end up as raw meat thrown to hungry lions. Fortunately, Tough Talk didn't end up as victims of a feeding time frenzy. Instead, they were met with a rare response. Respect. The muscles, the scars, the stories from the street: these bought valuable kudos with the assorted would-be hoodlums. The call-out kids stayed quiet. After initial unease at hearing the J-word, they listened with genuine interest. And when the dual demonstration of powerlifting and soul-baring was over, they were still quiet. They didn't riot as they left the room. They just filtered away, thinking.

In these days of inherited cynicism, young people don't often respond to the Christian message with ear and brain. There's something special about Tough Talk.

Yes, I thought as I contemplated a good night's sleep. There is something special about them. That's why I wrote that article – that's why I had wanted to tell my motormouth friend all about it. I made up my mind right then to call Arthur in the morning.

* * *

'Hello son, how are ya?' I'd managed to track Arthur down between gym visits.

'Good thanks. Just rang up to ask if you'd seen the article.'

'Yeah, I saw it. Very nice. Thanks.'

'Got anything else like that coming up?'

'Not really. We don't tend to spend much of our time in schools.'

Now this was difficult. I was fishing here, and I had a feeling that he knew it. There was no good reason for me to have phoned him – especially since he'd already sent me an e-mail to say thanks for the article and for the radio coverage I'd given to Tough Talk. Actually, I didn't really know why I was calling. There'd been this sixth-sense echo bouncing around my head for a while now, telling me in rebounding whispers that my part in the legend of King Arthur wasn't quite over yet. Unfortunately, there was nothing beyond that – no justification for investigating the same story again. I'd done Tough Talk hadn't I? Wasn't it time to move on to a pair of motor-racing vicars or something?

'How about the piece on the radio. Did you hear that?' (I'd played out a bit of my tape-recorded interview with Arthur which, transmitted on Medium Wave radio, sounded really top notch.)

'Yes, thanks son.'

Nope, that didn't help either. I sat silently on the end of the phone, praying that somehow a story would pop out of nowhere. And it was at this exact moment that I realised just how much I'd fallen in love. I'd spent years prior to this hoping that someone would prove my hunch that Christianity is relevant. I've grown up through church decline, moral decline, and the decline of the British situation comedy. I'm certain that the three are linked. . . . We're in an age now where people say they've no need for God anymore: that they can get by fine on their own, thank you very much. And faced with this awesome crisis in its global parish, the response from the church has been division, infighting, and retreat. I've always thought that by far the biggest problem with Christianity is that it's made up entirely of Christians.

'So . . . have you got anything exciting coming up?' I had the verbal shoehorn out now.

'Oh, lots. We should do about 250 missions and events this year.'

'Going anywhere nice?'

'Well, we're going to New York in May.'

Bingo. New York! Now that would be a story, I thought, as my mental typewriter went into overdrive. The Americans always inflict their preachers on us, but I wasn't sure I knew of too many instances of Britain returning the favour. I could interview them when they came back – they'd be sure to have a whole bunch of stories . . .

And then the typewriter jammed, and those two words tiptoed through my brain again, bringing with them a catalogue of library footage and history-etching screams. New York. The city which reluctantly played host to the day that changed the world.

'Really . . . ' I stumbled. 'You're going out to New York?'

'We're going to take a full team out there. We've been before, and they've invited us back to speak to some churches and run a couple of shows on the streets.

They're hurting pretty badly out there at the moment. They need something to believe in.'

Then, just as the conversation was about to end, Arthur said something: something insane, something I could never have expected him to ask. With eight short words he turned my life upside down.

'Why don't you come out there with us?'

* * *

Arthur's front room contains a lot of seating space. It's a testament to his friendly, welcoming character, and also to the size of some of his friends. In the centre of the room, three large sofas form a horseshoe-shaped shrine to community, so the average posterior is often spoilt for choice when its owner is told to 'sit down anywhere.'

Due to this abundance of upholstery, his long lounge often plays home to Tough Talk's weekly prayer meeting. After I'd accepted the New York proposal, Arthur and Ian had decided that it might be a good idea if I came along one week and met the whole team. I remember clearly – and it's important to recall this now – that Arthur definitely told me that it was a prayer meeting. 'We'll have some food, then we have a prayer meeting' – I'm sure that's what he'd said on the phone . . .

I arrived early at Arthur's house, where the great man was showing off culinary skills which subsequently proved to be quite substantial. With first option on every seat in the room I had a difficult decision to make, and whilst the champion powerlifter next door wrestled with half a ton of tuna, pasta and mayo, I allowed myself the luxury of trying the feel of several chairs. Eventually I settled on one end of a long leather sofa, and glanced around at the décor. On a sturdy shelf behind me, I noticed one of chef's trophies, which could perhaps only be described as thief-proof. Featuring a giant competitor with a heavily-loaded bar held comfortably aloft, this magnificent prize stood two feet tall, and was cast from solid iron. Thus, if ever a burglar was misinformed enough to attempt to procure the item from its solid home, the only thing he'd be leaving with would be a very serious hernia problem.

One by one, the members of Tough Talk filtered in, introduced themselves, then pondered the seating conundrum. For the duration of this period – which was about half an hour – I couldn't help feeling like the new kid in class. All eyes were on me – all minds were on trying to work out who I was. One of them got very twitchy and asked if I was an undercover policeman. Another cheekily asked if I'd got the wrong house. We all relaxed when I explained who I was and where I'd come from, although this did lead briefly to a barrage of questions on whether or not I knew their collective hero, a dulcet-toned features presenter by the name of Julia Fisher. I said that I knew her well, and I had them in my pocket. I was, it seemed, thanks to her, through the initiation.

Arthur re-entered, bearing three huge vats of high-car-bohydrate food. The assembled musclemen wasted no time in devouring it and, as the sofa showroom fell eeri-ly quiet, save for the deafening munch and crunch of a pack of hunger-crazed beasts, I took the opportunity to have a good look at each of them. To my left was Marcus, a tall man of West Indian descent, wrapped up in tight-fitting clothes and threatening to burst out of them with each robotic movement. Next to him was Steve, the ex-alcohol-fuelled knife-fighting football hooligan maniac, who was currently demonstrating about as much dining table etiquette as a JCB digger. By his side, not shovel-ling, was Ian McDowall, the founder and effectively the leader of Tough Talk, with whom I'd so far shared no conversation. Fork in hand, he simply looked back at me, smiling, letting me know that he could see what I was up to. I looked to the floor, and then on to the last three men: Arthur, slightly horrified by the rapid demise of his culinary craftsmanship; Adam, angular but more sensibly proportioned than the rest of the group, and Paul, who looked shiny, round and youthful. This was Tough Talk, all in one place, all struggling to fit within my field of vision. In the space of just those few moments, as I'd looked around a room, and simply turned my head from left to right, three vats of high-carbohydrate food had completely disappeared.

Crossing the room in confident strides, Ian squeezed in next to me and gave himself a proper introduction. He explained that his background was on a predictably awful par with Arthur's. Body-building was once the centre of his life . . . back then he was involved with the taking and dealing of illegal drugs . . . his marriage hit the rocks – in many ways he almost shared Arthur's story. But there were distinct differences. Apparently one of the key differences lay in the types of steroids they each used to use to enhance their muscles. By the sounds of things, Arthur's heart ballooning drugs were relatively tame.

'Do you know something?' belched Steve from across the foodless wasteland of the dining table. 'Ian used to take steroids that were supposed to be injected into horses. I've never seen him win a body-building competition, but he's won the Grand National three times.'

There was a ripple of laughter across the room. In his corner, Steve made several follow-up jokes involving sugar cubes, stables and blinkers, all of which were met with generous guffawing from the rest of the group. After a few generous smiles, Ian turned back to me and finished the story, with some illegal debt-collecting, the odd bit of nightclub door work and a sprinkling of armed violence. Then, with a smile which lit up his bulky frame and made him resemble a rather over-pumped James Bond, he asked me the question which I really didn't want him to ask.

'So what's your background then?'

Great. He tells me the kind of life story that would translate into a Hollywood script with ease, and then he expects me to follow it. I'm very tempted to lie and tell him that my dad is a Mafia hit man. Instead I tell him the truth, and feel a bit too squeaky-clean all of a sudden.

'Glad to have you on board for the New York trip' he said reassuringly. 'You can keep us all out of trouble. By the way, what exactly are you going to be doing out there with us?'

Good question Ian. Well done. Why didn't I think of that one? I didn't know why I was going to go out there – I thought Arthur had just invited me.

'I'm going to be making . . . a radio documentary . . . about your trip . . . ' I explained, with each word moving directly from imagination to mouth without a pause. 'I think . . . it's really interesting . . . how you're English . . . and going to America to evangelise . . . when normally it's the other way around.'

'Sounds good. Can't wait to hear it.'

And suddenly it all became very clear. Thanks to a sudden bout of generosity from Premier, my airfare had already been covered. It looked like I was going to be following this group of walking movie-pitches from London to New York, making a radio documentary along the way. Smiling with relief and a sense of belonging, I slid back into the sofa and waited for this long-delayed prayer meeting to begin.

Three quarters of an hour after the last Tough Talker had arrived we still hadn't started praying. Everyone was still busily exchanging tales from the gym, or from the carpentry trade, or from the kitchen. Occasionally there would be a moment of silence, but it was rarely more than thinking time before one of Steve's jokes, of which to be fair there were an excellent many. Informally my presence on the trip to America was mentioned and commended; informally the latest news from the charity was explained and discussed. And then suddenly, flicking like a light switch, Ian said:

'Right then, let's pray.'

Now I was ready for this, or at least I thought I was. Instinctively I assumed the position – fingers locked together, elbows pressed on to knees, head resting on hands (readily poised to sneakily sleep if the need arose). But around me I could sense something strange was going on. I realised, peeping through my fingers like a child in Sunday school, that I was the only person in the room who was sitting down. The rest were standing – some had even moved into a bit of space as if they were going to indulge in some impromptu star-jumps. Sheep-like I stood too, and then it started.

Until that precise moment, the word 'prayer' had always had a very narrow definition in my mind. To me 'prayer' meant small groups of old women spending hours in silence; a young eloquent poet reading from a sheet with his best Noel Coward voice; a child muttering thankyous to the creator of the universe for her jam sandwich. It didn't mean shouting vehemently, speaking at the same time as everyone else, or suddenly being fluent in a strange foreign language. Until that moment.

'A prayer meeting' – again, I was sure that's what he'd said on the phone. Surely some mistake then? Ian vociferates with potentially perfect pronunciation, in the kind of tongue that's usually heard by lost safari tourists. Then Arthur cuts across him, bellowing out some passage from the Bible. Then Marcus says what I'd consider to be a more conventional prayer, but at twelve times the usual volume. Then Arthur starts everyone off in a song. Meanwhile I'm back in my chair, now switched to the shampoo position with hands wrapped across the top of my head. I'll be honest – I was scared, and I was fighting it. And then I heard my name mentioned – then I heard Arthur:

'We want to pray for Martin, Lord . . . '

A massive chorus of approval rose up from within the room.

'We want to ask you to bless him Lord – bless his family, bless his job. Look after him Lord . . . '

Another chorus, even more massive.

'Touch him with your Holy Spirit, fill him with your love Lord . . . '

I don't know when I stopped fighting, or fearing, or clasping my head so tightly. Maybe it was that affirming chorus that kept going up whenever my name was mentioned, or maybe all the shouting had just anaesthetised me a little. Yet as Arthur's assertive words went heavenwards, I started to feel a lot more comfortable with prayer the Tough Talk way.

Then, suddenly, I believe that God gave me a little wake-up call. I started to feel like something was moving between my shoulder blades, and down through my spine. Something warm, and slightly ticklish, but fuzzy, inexplicable, unlike anything else. It wasn't backache, it wasn't tiredness, it wasn't sickness – just a real feeling that I couldn't explain but which felt very, very good. I'm not going to claim that the Holy Spirit knocked me to the floor, made me fly around the room or taught me Mandarin, but I do believe that in that moment he gave me a little hug. And I felt genuine physical warmth, and genuine emotional peace. It was a supernatural experience of the most gentle and honest kind – I sat quietly in the corner, and God chose to touch me. At that moment, something became very clear to me. God was with these people.

Just as suddenly as it had begun, the Tough Talk prayer meeting snapped to a halt. There was a moment of silence, as each man said a spiritual farewell in his head, and then the chairs were full again, the conversation restarted where it had left off, and Arthur sidled up alongside me.

'You alright?' he asked, remembering too late that I was not from a Pentecostal background.

'Yes. I'm fine thanks. That was an experience,' I chuckled.

He chuckled too. Then he flipped his diary open in front of me.

'At the start of April, we're taking a team over to France. Just for a weekend, near the Swiss border. How would you feel about the idea of coming with us?'

France now? I should spend some more time with these guys, I thought. I'll be getting my passport stamped more often than Phileas Fogg. Buoyed by the freshness of my recent spiritual encounter, I allowed my deliberations to last no more than a split-second.

'I'd love to – that'll make the documentary even better.' Besides, I needed a holiday, and that mountain air sounded pretty persuasive to me.

So, one month after watching three former no-hopers lift weights in a school hall, I was now gearing myself up for a journey which would take in the French Alps and the world's most infamous city. And within a couple more flips of Arthur's diary, I'd pencilled in another stop in Manchester, and a trip to the British Powerlifting Championships. This was turning into something of an adventure.

Chapter 3

Soulever Avec Puissance

7.31 a.m. Three small iced cakes

The 650 miles that separate deepest darkest Essex from the glorious mountains of the French–Swiss border are best traversed from several thousand feet. Unfortunately, when you want to take 250 kilos of weightlifting equipment in your hand luggage, the long and winding road becomes the only sensible option. Thus, when Tough Talk decided to hit the continent one warm April morning, they packed up the Transit van, squeezed their ample frames inside, and made me the jammed-in filling of a muscle doughnut. Rolling out of Loughton at an unfeasibly antisocial hour, we embarked upon a journey that was unlikely to end in daylight.

9.12 a.m. One Double Whopper with cheese

As we made our way around the choking collar of congestion that Londoners refer to as 'the devil's road', I took time to examine my closer-than-comfort back-seat companions. Competing with the left side of my body for the little seating space it occupied, a tanned, squat lump of human bulk sat munching, chewing and guzzling the morning away. On my right, a smaller, but still muscular chap lay still and silent, busied with dreams of the adventure to come. His dark glasses didn't fool me for long. This was the first nap of the day for him, and the first of many.

11.35 a.m. Tuna sandwiches, four rounds, on thick bread

The snoring ginger-mopped sloth is Adam McMillan, official roadie to Tough Talk and notorious ex-thief. The food monster, who goes to great lengths to explain that his constant grub-processing is due to natural energy requirements rather than barefaced gluttony, is Paul De Freitas. Both are established members of the team; both live in a gym; both need more room than one-third of a van seat can offer.

12.30 p.m. Twix bar

In command of the vehicle were a husband and wife combination who'd diplomatically divided wheel-turning and map-reading responsibilities. Arthur took the helm, and whilst keeping his eyes on the road, gave his passengers a constant series of glimpses into the huge storybook in his brain. Before we'd reached the Channel Tunnel, we'd already heard about the time he dumped six heavy goods vehicles in a gravel pit, and the day he blew up the wrong Jaguar. At least with Arthur on board, traffic jams and repetitive miles of scenery would pass a little more quickly. By his side sat wife Jacqui, although as an impartial observer who'd heard the family history, I found it quite difficult to understand why.

12.50 p.m. One biscuit (chocolate); one orange

When Paul isn't eating, he's generally singing. He's proud of the fact that he belts out backing vocals with a local covers band, and it became painfully clear during much of this afternoon that he likes to spend a lot of his time practising. Early in the day, Arthur gave Paul a musical idea that would have serious aural repercussions for the rest of us. In another bout of tale-telling and light conversation, he'd explained his personal penchant for rewriting popular East-End songs with spiritual lyrics. When Arthur is in full voice, 'Maybe it's because I'm a Londoner' becomes 'Maybe it's because I'm a Christian.' 'I'm forever blowing bubbles' changes to 'I'm forever praising Jesus.' Clearly Mr White has a gift of pure creative genius, the like of which arguably has not been seen since the days of Shakespeare.

Inspired by the sheer poetry, Paul proceeded to spend the next three hours in a musical journey through most of the classic popular music of the last five decades, replacing all the two-syllable words in the lyrics with 'Jesus'.

1.55 p.m. Two cheese and cucumber sandwiches

The constant tunes of the happy eater sent me into a somewhat transient state, and I found time to reflect on a rather bizarre experience from the night before. The prospect of going away into the mission field had made me feel a bit super-spiritual, and I felt the urge to go miracle hunting. So, after arriving once again at Loughton underground station, I'd chosen not to call Arthur for another lift, and instead had decided to find my own way to his house through trial and error.

I had only been to White Towers twice before, and on neither occasion was I taking the slightest bit of interest in the route that we'd driven. Yet after a short prayer and fifteen minutes of clueless marching, I'd found my way to the correct front door without taking a single wrong turn. Hardly a miracle of biblical proportions I know, but a good start to the weekend.

2.15 p.m. Three Murray Mints

Adam was continuing to drift in and out of the land of the living; Paul was busy singing with his mouth full. Around a hundred miles into France, a visit to a service station offered a brief respite from their bad habits.

3.09 p.m. Chicken, breast of; second orange

After the realisation that everyone in France speaks French had dawned on our party, and our inability to do likewise had prevented us from buying any more food for Paul, Arthur decide to regale us with a few stories from the strange world of powerlifting. By far the most interesting was the tale of a female lifter whom Arthur had befriended some years earlier.

Apparently, this young lady's addiction to muscle-enhancing steroids had a rather unpleasant side effect, which caused her body to produce a masculine amount of facial hair. Although this by no means improved her looks, the steroids began to have a definite effect on her muscles, and she made the decision to live with the growth. After time of course, shaving cream and a razor became as integral a part of her daily routine as the bench-press and the deadlift.

One day, this new experience set in motion a train of thought with an unthinkable destination. Mrs Stubble began to wonder, if she didn't shave, just how prolific her facial hair might become. So, when her seafaring husband set off on a three-month voyage, she decided to lock all her grooming equipment in the cupboard, and head for a log cabin hideaway where she could spend ninety days *au naturel*.

Unfortunately, her other half was involved in an accident on the open waves, and was sent home with his arm in plaster. Buoyed by the upside of his misfortune, he decided to return to his darling wife in secret and surprise her. Finding their home empty, he traced her route to the woodland hideaway and, with a bouquet in his good hand, finally arrived to knock at her door. When it opened, she appeared – two months into her reclusion – with a full beard and bushy moustache. Needless to say, the broken sailor turned, ran, and never stopped running.

'Steroids ruin people's lives' said Arthur, although he didn't need to.

4.30 p.m. Doughnut, portion of

Tough Talk are a group of men who speak only in English and, furthermore, only a certain derivative form of standard English which even I have some trouble understanding. Brought up in a community that insisted on burying bad poetry at the heart of its dialect, Arthur & Co. are never happier than when they're resting their 'plates of meat' in the 'rub-a-dub.' So as we stopped at a service station in the warm mid-afternoon, I couldn't help but wonder about the implications of the language barrier.

The French, on the other hand, are well known for their cosmopolitan culture, where fluency in a second language is a prerequisite. Notoriously though, many French people make the decision not to communicate in English, even if they can, for the simple reason that they don't wish to encourage British laziness any further. The only way around this, as I discovered over the following few days, is to make an effort, however embarrassing, at addressing them first in a potholed version of their own language. At this point, in almost every scenario, the barrier is lowered and communication can begin. Usually, all that's required of the ignorant Brit in this diplomatic negotiation is a *Bonjour* and a couple of *Mercis*. Regrettably, as we headed towards another expensive

toll booth on this giant metal snake through the country-
side, even these simple sound formations seemed to be
too much for the boys. On my left, Paul could master 'my
name is . . . ' but only when he repeated it after me. On
my right, still wedged, but at last awake, Adam was having a lot of trouble with pronunciation. The speed with
which good French words, when placed on his tongue,
twisted and transformed in both sound and meaning
was quite staggering. If he were to walk into a shop and
order a cup of coffee, it's very likely he'd be given directions to a car park. Meanwhile in the front of the van, as
Arthur played dumb, Jacqui's love of the sitcom '*Allo*
'*Allo* was coming flooding back. Our survival, and our
ability to buy food for Paul over the next few days was
very likely to rely on her quite heavily.

'We're going to stop for a coffee,' said Arthur.

'*Fanatique*,' said Adam.

5.35 p.m. Three full-fat chocolate biscuits

At the turn of the last century, Britain was sending missionaries out to far-flung corners of the globe, on cramped
ships and camel trips. West Africa, South America, the
Gobi Desert: nowhere was safe from the message of the
cross, as long as it was thousands of miles away and
incredibly difficult for a middle-class white person to survive in. It probably never crossed the minds of those men
and women, as they clutched their Bibles and marched
forward in truth and righteousness, that all that reaping
and sowing could just have easily gone on right on their
doorstep. Yet now, a hundred years later, these modern
missionaries were travelling for just a few hours to get to
their mission field, to a place where the Christian message
was rarely heard and seldom preached.

'This isn't just about what you see' said Arthur suddenly.

Adam woke again. Paul stopped eating, albeit briefly.

'There'll be more going on this weekend than meets the eye. This place we're going to, this town Châtel, has never heard about Jesus Christ. That's why we're going. You know, normally when we stand on some steps or in a market square and talk about God, we know that someone else has almost certainly stood there before us; that years ago, Wesley or someone similar had ridden up on his horse and preached to the people. When we tell people our stories, we know that at some point in history, someone else had stood on that spot and done the same. Well it's not like that this time. This time we become the first people ever to stand in that town and say the things that we have to say about God. That's why we're going to France. That's why we've driven all this way, cramped up in this van on this boring great road. Because Jesus Christ is real, and because no one has told the people of this town.'

Arthur loves the speeches of Winston Churchill. I'm reliably informed that he has many of the 'greats' in his record collection at home. When Arthur talks about evangelism – about going out and telling people about his life and his beliefs – he assumes a lot of that great man's speechmaking prowess. As he explained, heart on sleeve, his reasons for coming out here, I half expected him to close with the words of Churchill himself:

'And we will go out to Châtel. And we will tell them the truth about Jesus Christ. And we will never, ever, ever surrender . . . '

6.41 p.m. 28 Ritz cheese biscuits

Adam, forced to remain awake by a recurring nightmare that Paul was going to eat him, finally proved that there was more to him than tiredness as light began to fade across the continent. Before the evening, the only

story he'd told had been about his last visit to the south-
east coast of England, where he'd been questioned by
police over a local murder. On the basis of that snapshot,
I'd pretty much convinced myself that it was better to let
him sleep. However, as the growing darkness rather per-
versely shook him into life, and he began to tell me his
story, I saw a different side. And I saw his eyes for the
first time.

Long ago, back in Adam's dim and distant past, he
used to define himself as a thief. Bereft of a full-time job,
he'd while away his days robbing factories and yards,
and cruise through his evenings stealing expensive motor
cars. He was a walking photo-fit; the kind of person about
whom the police would run advertising campaigns. But
by his own standards at the time, he wasn't a bad person.
Inside his head, he'd established his own twisted moral
code in order to evade those inevitable feelings of guilt.
For instance, he was incredibly careful to only steal brand
new cars – the kind which he felt sure would still be heavily insured. By implementing this strategy, and thus robbing from insurance companies rather than directly from
the man on the street, he was able to maintain a clear con-
science at all times.

One day, possibly in contravention of this self-
imposed rulebook, he and an associate broke into and
robbed a local church. After smashing their way through
a huge oak door, they cracked the safe, swiped the offering, and bag-bundled all of the silverware. This, according to a still embarrassed Adam, was possibly the lowest
point of his career as a low-life. Nevertheless, petty crime
remained his raison d'être.

Four years later, a leaflet explaining the Christian faith
popped through the letterbox of Adam's criminal lair. He
was getting pretty fed up of being 'bad' by that time, and
had even started to question his misshapen morals. For

the last couple of years, Adam had been taking the Bible
to bed anyway – albeit with a can of beer in one hand and
a spliff in the ashtray. This piece of paper, which in most
homes would have immediately found itself in the dust-
bin, had arrived at just the right moment. The leaflet itself
was a pretty standard affair, stating the problem with
mankind and the answer, to be supposedly found above,
and concluding with a quick fill-your-name-in-here
prayer for instant repentance. But for Adam it represen-
ted a good argument and a good idea. Filling in the blank
with a ballpoint pen, Adam prayed the prayer, felt
instantly guilty about his cumulative badness, and vowed
never to commit so much as a parking offence ever again.

A few days later, Adam realised that Christians generally go to church. The leaflet people had helpfully provided a few local addresses, and so that Sunday, Adam
followed directions to the first name on the list. And as
he walked through the huge, broken door he realised, as
we all occasionally do, that God would make a great
scriptwriter. Irony of ironies, Adam was standing in the
same church that he'd broken into, four years earlier.

He told me all this, like he tells everyone else, and I
gasped and giggled in all the right places, just like all his
other audiences probably do. Stories like his make you
think.

7.32 p.m. Barbecued chicken leg; another Murray Mint

We paid a final, huge toll to gain entry to an adventure
playground of French B-roads, just as Ian McDowall and
his family touched down in comfort at Geneva airport.
Exhausted by five minutes of talking, Adam again began
to sink into his seat, lullabied by Paul's newly rewritten
'Jesus B. Goode'.

'Ian!' exclaimed Arthur at his mobile phone. 'How are
you son?'

Ian told him, although since this is a true story, I've no way of knowing what he said.

'Yeah, it's been great,' replied Arthur to the phone after a while. 'I've had hour-long trips around the M25 that have seemed longer.'

I thought about this: about Arthur's ridiculous claim that a trip of more than half a day could seem shorter and easier than one of sixty minutes. He was right. The banter, the singing, the laughter that we'd enjoyed all the way along had actually made this cramped up journey enjoyable. In our repeated trips to the service stations, tollbooths and roadside toilets of France, we'd been introduced to a new culture. In our constant rota of storytelling we'd all made at least one new friend. It'd been an eye-opening trip so far for all of us in one way or another, even for Adam, who'd barely had his eyes open. So as the phone call ended, and I pictured Ian fighting through customs, baggage reclaim and a mile-long taxi queue, I suddenly stopped feeling sorry for my squashed up legs, and felt thankful for having shared the experience.

9.20 p.m. Sponge cake, regular size; four chunks of chocolate; three handfuls of ready salted potato chips

We reached a moonlit Châtel just after nine, and on jelly legs found our way to the waiting accommodation. Inside we met Ian, his wife Valerie and his 13-year-old Jenga champion daughter Bianca. Alongside Ian stood his brother Lloyd: a tall handsome man who I assumed had invited the Tough Talk team out here. I assumed wrong.

10.01 p.m. Brie on toast, four thick slices; extra sponge cake

After I'd spent most of the day tightly packed between Adam and Paul, the news of our sleeping arrangements seemed fitting. I contemplated the steep steps down to 'the cave' – the sleeps-three basement bedroom beneath the chalet – but paused on hearing a series of crashing sounds below. My two evangelist friends, their muscles rippling in the glare of the nightlights, were wrestling with some viciousness over the rights to the bottom bunk. Designed and built, like the whole of the chalet, by another of Ian's brothers, this room was fitted with two wall-mounted beds and a third beneath. On entering the premises, Paul had immediately noted that the space left between these top-bunks and the ceiling were best suited to a child, and not a man with the limbs of an elephant. Therefore, he was willing to go to great lengths to ensure his presence on the bottom, and decided to impress the point on Adam. I only thank God that I stopped off upstairs to brush my teeth, or it could have been me.

The friendly disagreement subsided and, with some difficulty, the three of us took to our bunks. Returning again to his natural field of expertise, Adam mumbled something about getting up early, before swiftly expiring for the day. Paul moaned softly that he'd not had any dinner before doing likewise. Then silence.

* * *

I awoke to an incredible mountain view, although a little earlier than I'd hoped. I discovered to my cost that the key to Adam's all-day-long sleepiness was in fact his reluctance to spend a good number of hours in the sack at night. He's a late-to-bed, early-to-rise kind of guy and, in this respect at least, is the worst kind of roommate. It was his bright idea to take Paul and Ian for a crack-of-dawn exploratory visit to the town, and to wake me up on his way out. 6 a.m. was not my idea of a holiday lie-in. In fact, I was originally woken an hour earlier, thanks to Adam's inability to understand the time difference.

At around nine, the wanderers returned from their recce armed with milk, croissants and one very amusing story. Our chalet was set on the side of a mountain, at the foot of which stood the town centre. On the previous night, Ian's brother Lloyd had advised us that there was a quicker way to get down there than on the long road which wound back and forth across the mountainside. This more direct route took the form of a path, which was, in his opinion, fairly steep but quite manageable. On their morning trek, the boys were unable to find said path, and were about to tackle the longer, more winding option, when Paul's adventurous instincts kicked in. He spotted a path-of-sorts, which seemed to head in the direction of the town and, despite the protestations of his companions, led them all onward. It may have struck some people to turn back when they encountered barbed wire, but not Paul. He was sure that this was the right way. And once they had clambered over that trap, and watched Adam's new trousers suffer a large tear, and then been confronted by a near-vertical drop that closely resembled a cliff face, they would have been forgiven for calling for help. Again, not Paul. He was still sure that this was the right way. And so it was that Paul, Adam and Ian said 'good morning' to Châtel by running down a mountain slope that most Olympians would refuse to ski down.

Lloyd, one of Ian's many siblings, introduced himself properly as we sat down to eat a full English breakfast (when in Rome? *Sacré bleu!*). Explaining that he owned the chalet above ours, he told us that, just six months previously, he had made the biggest decision of his life. With a pretty wife and a young family in tow, he'd uprooted everything and swapped the London smog for the idyllic peaks that now surrounded us. From where I was

standing, that didn't seem like too difficult a decision
actually. On all four sides, huge snow-smothered mountains loomed like the roofless walls of God's playpen.
There were ski slopes; there were huge evergreens; there
were people – smiling, croissant-chomping people,
wherever you cared to look. If a combination of sun and
snow are the benchmark, this place was little short of
paradise on earth.

I was surprised to learn however, that Lloyd was not,
as I had foolishly assumed, a Christian. Nor, as I had also
taken for granted, had he invited Tough Talk to come out
here. He was pleased to see Ian, for sure, but he didn't
ask him to come. The two factors – Lloyd's presence here
and ours – were, in fact, totally unconnected. Which was
confusing, since Châtel is a small town in the middle of
nowhere.

Lloyd left us to eat, and as I munched on my bacon,
and Paul munched on little Bianca's, Ian told tales of how
not to evangelise. It seemed that where Christianity was
concerned, he had rather alienated his brother with an
unhelpful burst of post-conversion exuberance. He
admitted, a little ashamedly, that he'd come on a little
strong when initially explaining his new-found faith:

'I basically didn't talk to him about anything else for
months. You know how it is, when you're excited about
something don't you?'

Various people grunted affirmingly through mouth-
fuls of fresh French *oeuf*.

'Well I had all this excitement just burning away inside
of me. I just wanted to tell everyone, and I didn't want to
take no for an answer.'

Ian's wife, reclining out of shot with a moderate bowl
of cereal, giggled knowingly.

'But he really wasn't interested, and I should have
given him a bit of space.'

'So when did you give up?' I asked.

'Well, there was this time when we were coming out of the gym together and I was telling him about my faith again. And I kept talking, on and on about the same thing, while he got into his car. In the end he just drove off, leaving me yapping at the side of the road. I think that was the moment I realised that I needed to ease off a bit.'

Valerie giggled again. But Ian was suddenly serious.

'I'm hoping to put things right this weekend,' he said softly. 'It'd be nice if he could come and see Tough Talk, to understand what we actually do. I think I gave him a bad impression of what Christianity's all about. And I guess deep down I'm hoping he'll see the truth of what we're talking about. But really I just want him to come and see what we do.'

And he said a little prayer to that effect, which would be answered approximately four hours later.

Tough Talk had actually been invited to France by Snow Peak, a ski holiday company with a Christian bias. Their base, in downtown Châtel, became our mission control centre for the next two days, and was home to a number of particularly helpful characters: Gene and Katherine, the hospitable Canadian housekeepers; Tall Paul, the resident spiritual guru; and an assortment of bemused holidaymakers from Blighty. For an hour that afternoon we sat in these comfortable log cabin surroundings, quaffing coffee and biting biscuits, and I began to wonder whether this was supposed to be an outreach or a holiday. Gene enthused about the Tough Talk video he'd seen, and Tall Paul bemoaned the state of the French church. We continued to dunk and drink for some time.

The mood changed, however, with the arrival of a Frenchman. History is littered with examples of this of course, but today's Napoleon was just a little man from down the road: Luc Favre, a pastor from a nearby town and Tough Talk translator for the day. A slightly built thirtysomething with a young family around his ankles, he was currently in the process of setting up an Evangelical church in Thonon, less than forty miles to the west of Châtel. He spoke better English than any of us.

The plan today was to take the Tough Talk show out onto the streets of the town. As Arthur had explained in the previous day's driving marathon, this was the first time that anything of this kind had ever been attempted out here, due to a combination of spiritual apathy and legal implications. It is apparently against the law to preach on public property in France, and whilst contravening these regulations might not lead us to a night in the cells, any attempt to put on a show in the street would be closed down as quickly as it had begun. Thankfully, the locals had discovered a workable loophole to the rules, in that it was perfectly legal for someone to preach to the public, as long as they didn't set foot on public property when doing so. Thus a search had been carried out to find a suitable shop, house or pizza joint in the vicinity which would happily allow a group of Englishmen to lift weights on their premises. The unlikely saviour had appeared in the shape of Pippo, a local restaurateur whose popular establishment was situated at the foot of the main ski slopes. He wasn't a Christian, but felt simply that 'the kids around here need something to believe in.'

Luc expressed his embarrassment at his own poor English by using a number of four-syllable words which I only learned during a University English degree. Ian expressed his embarrassment at his own poor French by unsuccessfully counting to three. Despite his modesty, Luc would make an excellent translator, as long as Ian veered away from the use of cockney rhyming slang when telling his story. The confusion caused among a watching French crowd, as Luc translated 'this bloke half-inched me motor so I give him one in the boat race', would surely have been too great.

'I am very excited to be 'elping you today' proclaimed Luc through his twenty-five letter alphabet. 'But I am concerned I may make a mistake. I lived in England for 'alf a year, but I 'ave not done many translations before.'

'That's alright, just make it up as you go along,' Arthur only half-joked as he drained his coffee cup.

'It 'eez very important to me. The message you bring 'as never been spoken in our part of France. People 'ave been praying for someone to come 'ere and do eet for many years.'

(This, I later discovered, was completely true, and possibly connected to Arthur Churchill's 'more to this mission than meets the eye' speech. Ten years before our arrival here, a group of Christians had begun to meet and pray that one day, missionaries from overseas would come to Châtel and talk about Jesus on the streets. Maybe it was the decimal perfection of the timescale involved, or just the good feeling that was now being breathed towards us from all directions, but I found that pretty staggering actually.)

For the next twenty minutes Ian and Arthur indulged in some of their paint-stripper prayer – this time I was prepared, but I can't vouch for some of the unsuspecting tourists. Luc seemed to be in on the game too, although it was hard to tell whether he was praying in tongues at all, or just using French words in advance of the GCSE syllabus. But while last time I'd been a little taken aback by this approach to addressing God, this time around I was prepared. I even did a bit of shouting of my own. And it seemed to me that part of the reason that Tough

Talk shout and scream in prayer (aside from the fact that this is how they worship), is that they genuinely care about what they are praying. So often I've sat in church and heard an old man drone on about 'saving the lost' and 'ending injustice.' But somehow, sentiments like that seem so much more heartfelt and meaningful when blasted out at 100 decibels.

After the prayer meeting, I took the opportunity to interview Luc for the Premier Radio documentary. Over the course of the next few weeks, I'd meet lots of people, and try to get a few words from nearly all of them. So to save you from having to hear about it every time it happened, just take it as read that whenever I was with Tough Talk, that's what I was doing – interviewing, editing and making copious notes. Fill in the blanks yourself, because as I said before, I'm not important in this story.

Half an hour later, after a minibus journey that took in the sights of Châtel, including a 200-foot waterfall and a cliff face which seemed oddly memorable to Ian, Adam and Paul, we arrived at the 'promised land'. Again, snow-covered, tree-covered mountains angled upwards in every direction. Hundreds of people on skis and seats, enjoying the piste or a few glasses of wine, went about the business of a contented town. And in the centre of the action, busy and bustling, was Tough Talk's pavement pulpit. With all hands on deck, we struggled across to it with weights, bars and public address equipment. The chunky-but-cheerful restaurant owner bid us welcome, and assorted locals scowled like stereotypes from a xenophobic comedy. A general air of *qu'est ce que c'est* (or 'what-on-earth') descended all around us. It seemed we were guaranteed a crowd, even if we couldn't be sure of a friendly one.

Adam and Paul marked out a plot of land about ten metres square. In two corners, speakers were placed on metal stalks, ready to blast the unsuspecting wine drinkers with unwelcome dance music. A weightlifting bench took centre stage, along with an immovable quantity of pressed rubber weights. Along some near-by railings, a huge black and red Tough Talk banner was unfurled. Two microphones were put in place, in preparation for the forthcoming bilingual assault. And after a quick agreement on the word 'ready', the show began.

'Hello Châtel!' shouted Arthur, with a cheeky excite-ment at the thought that he was about to be translated. To be fair, even he might have managed this one.

'*Bonjour Châtel!*' smiled Luc. This was easy.

'We're a group of men from England called Tough Talk.'

Cue pause. Cue authentic-sounding translation.

'We haven't come here to teach or preach to you; to patronise or talk down to you.'

Cue Luc – still going strong.

'But we've come to tell you some good news, and about how our lives were changed.'

Cue translation. Cue sceptical looks from locals.

'We've come to lift some weights, but most of all we've come all the way from England to tell you the truth about Jesus Christ, and how he can change your lives like he's changed ours.'

Cue Luc. Cue large noticeable reaction at the mention of the word 'Jesus'.

An almost instantly-formed crowd, which had semi-circled around the cabaret, took a full step backwards in eerie unison as that name was uttered. Thankfully they didn't disperse, perhaps because they were being glued together by a few friendly faces. One belonged to Gene;

one belonged to Tall Paul; and one, much to Ian's delight, belonged to Lloyd.

After dropping the J-word bombshell, it was time for a little showmanship. This is how Tough Talk work: they start talking, then they interrupt themselves with the weights, then they talk again, and so on. The evangelist's rulebook, as used by street corner nutcases everywhere, clearly states that all sermons should be started and then finished, without interruption if possible. Tough Talk's copy may have a page missing somewhere.

So to give Luc a little break, Ian took up position under the lightly loaded bar and began bench-pressing. Lying flat on the padded black seat, he lifted the bar up and down above his chest in the kind of controlled movement that wouldn't have looked out of place at ballet school. It didn't weigh very much, but the chunky rubber weights and Ian's sun-moistened forehead helped to improve the picture. Anyhow, the surrounding tourists, restaurateurs and family-members were transfixed. One quick burst of Arthur and Luc later, it was their turn to have a go. Now if this had been attempted in England, perhaps in a busy shopping centre in Leeds or Manchester, a stooge or two would presently have been required. An assembly of Brits who had for the last few minutes been hanging on every word and following every lift, would now be casting thousand-yard stares into the distance, or nervously fumbling in their Gap bags. Fortunately, this was holiday-heaven France, where stresses are low and fun is top of the agenda. The warm air and pretty scenery act as a permanent masseur to everyone there. So, since this was not a Manchester shopping centre on a wet Saturday afternoon, volunteers were forthcoming.

Now this, you have to hand it to them, was clever. No crowd is going to walk away when one of their own has become part of the show. And as before, their often-feeble attempts to outlift one another were broken up by a few more life-changing words from Arthur. So Tough Talk had a captive audience, emotionally chained to the spot and listening to the message as they waited for the next opportunity to cheer on their friends. Very sneaky.

As the lifting action warmed up, so did Arthur's story. He talked about the drugs (or rather Luc did), then he talked about his affair (although not too much as there were children present), and then he talked about the violence. The crowd, a steady group now of forty or so individuals, were enthralled. But this gives a rather false impression of how many people were actually listening. Behind the lifting area, afternoon skiers were making their way off the *piste* with remarkable sluggishness. The removal of skis from the feet, which would normally take a minute or so, was somehow taking ten. Behind us, in the forecourt of Pippo's restaurant, unusually large groups of people were enjoying a drawn out coffee. As we'd always known, it wasn't socially acceptable over here to be seen standing and listening to this sort of thing and these sorts of people. But from a certain distance, it was merely an unfortunate accident if you happened to overhear them.

This time, as Arthur's story reached its conclusion, the J-word provoked only half a backward step from the watching public. And as he signed off with his regular 'you can say what you like about me but you cannot deny the truth of my life' there were even gentle nods of agreement. They seemed satisfied that his life had miraculously changed – after all, he sounded like a pretty honest and believable fellow. They were unconvinced however, that the Tough Talk-branded New Testaments which he offered to them with such great gusto, contained the real reasons behind that change. No one

accepted the free literature (which was in English anyway), but Arthur was unperturbed.

'We'll be lifting some more weights in about five minutes,' announced Luc, before magically making the
crowd vanish into thin mountain air.

Adam and Paul are humble men. One of them may be
the Incredible Sleeping Man and one of them may
be hungrier than a champion racehorse, but I'm pleased
to report, after spending a fair amount of time with
them, that these are their only major vices. And so
neither of them is too proud, too arrogant, too self-
important to simply operate as a cog in the Tough Talk
wheel. All Adam usually does at an event such as this is
to load and unload the bar, and to pack and unpack the
van. He does it quietly, and with a smile on his face. And
although his contribution may seem small, he adds a
much-needed spirit of teamwork to what is essentially
a team. He has what fans of Christian jargon like to call
'a servant heart'.

Paul was due to lift as part of the demonstration, but
bizarrely, as they have 'the wrong type of gravel' in
Châtel, his particular specialist discipline would have
been too dangerous. So, while Ian and Arthur shared
speaking and lifting duties (or 'the important stuff'),
Paul simply had to help Adam with the loading and
moving. He too got on with the job; he too smiled. In the
afternoon sun, and in the kind of scenery that inspired
the Von Trapps to sing, one thing amazed and warmed
me more than anything else: the genuine attitudes of two
lads who really had just come out to serve their God. So
as I said: Adam and Paul are humble men.

Another blast of music assembled a second crowd:
wide-eyed, fresh-faced, and ready to be offended by

five-letter words. This time it was Ian's turn on the microphone.

'*Bonjour Châtel,*' he smiled. Then, unfortunately, he tried too hard and fell off the slippery language-log that he should never have attempted to traverse:

'*Je m'appelle Tough Talk!*' He smiled again. Puzzled looks stung at him from numerous angles, as the new crowd attempted to process 'My name is Tough Talk.' He didn't look much like a Red Indian from where they were standing.

'I used to be a nightclub doorman in the East End of London' he explained, thankfully reverting to Standard English. Then he and the ever-ready Luc told his story: a tale of fights, weapons, blood and salvation. Again, as Jesus Christ entered the equation, the onlookers were unsure whether to smile in agreement or grimace in disgust. But whatever they were thinking, Lloyd included, at least they were thinking. In a reversal of Act I, Ian's blood-soaked storytelling was chequered by Arthur-led powerlifting, complete with more audience participation. And this time, in a beautiful act of family reconciliation, even Lloyd joined in the fun. Ian spoke, then his brother lifted, and there was joy in both their faces. If he achieved nothing else all weekend, he had at least convinced his brother that he wasn't completely mad after all.

In fact this soap-opera style moment of brotherly love was so touching, that I almost didn't notice what was going on centre-stage. Luc, who had gamely translated the cockney dialect to the best of his ability, was suddenly a picture of emotion. He wasn't grinning from ear to ear, nor were there tears in his eyes. But the man was positively glowing, like an overcharged battery. And as he stood and translated the last of Ian's God-focused words, it struck me between the eyes. Luc, the passionate clergyman, was standing on the streets of his native France and screaming out the name of Jesus Christ – the God on whom he'd based his whole world. He'd probably never done this before in his life – and thanks to government loopholes, nobody could stop him now. When Ian finished, I fully expected Luc to continue preaching long after the microphone had been switched off.

That night, as we took our places at what we were reliably informed (by the owner) was the best table in France, Ian and I talked formally about the mission. Even though I was here in my own time, independently of my job, Ian refused to address me as if I was a regular member of the public, or even a friend. Whether this was because he was nervous of journalists, or because I was the kind of chubby, mouthy idiot that he'd have turned away from one of his nightclub doors, I didn't know. Anyway, conversations with Ian in Châtel (he got better later) always felt a bit like an interview. Basically, he thought very carefully about his words and tried to speak entirely in soundbites, while I did a lot of nodding and prodding.

'Ian,' I started, after explaining what the menu meant and being commendably honest about l'escargot. 'I've got to ask you this. You came out here on a Christian mission, right?'

'Right.'

'And the idea is to convert people to Christianity, right?'

'Usually, yes.'

'Oh.' My line of questioning was flawed, I could feel it already. Nevertheless, I'd started so I'd finish. 'Well you didn't get any converts today, did you. And yet you're all smiling.'

'Yes. Because this is a very different thing we're doing out here. Usually when we do a Tough Talk on the streets, we'd be inviting the people in the crowd along to

an event. The local church would put on an evening
meeting, or a breakfast, and we'd go along and do a
longer, harder-hitting presentation there. And at the end
of that, we'd ask people if they want to know Jesus
Christ. But this isn't like that. This whole mission is
based around an open-air presentation in an area that's
never heard the gospel preached in the open air. There is
a little church in this town, but it's so steeped in religion
and religiousness that it doesn't really understand what
the gospel of Jesus is all about. So I believe that, more
importantly than what we'll actually see achieved, it'll be
a spiritual statement for this region – that at long last
people have preached the gospel here on the streets. So
our hope is just to break some new ground, in a spiritual
sense. We always knew that we weren't going to see
much fruit on this particular mission – it was more about
sowing some seeds, and trying to be obedient to what
God wanted us to do. I think there's more to all this than
what we've seen with our eyes. We'll do a mission in
New York and see a hundred people come to know the
Lord, and you can see the fruit there and then. But I
believe that bigger things – spiritual things – have gone
on here, and all we needed to do was be obedient. And
sometimes with things like this you never know quite
what you've done, and you might never know the real
purpose of why God's called you out there.'

All this talk of fruit and seeds had made Paul hungry.
Luckily, the end of Ian's little speech coincided with the
arrival of dinner. The meal – adventurously I gambled on
the steak and *frites* – was delivered by a tall skinny
French waiter who seemed to be even better at English
than Luc. These people really knew how to rub our ignorant British noses in it.

As he delivered Arthur's specially enlarged portion of
meat and potato, I caught the waiter staring enviously at

the four heavily worked-out bodies at our table. Suddenly, possessed by some unknown force, I felt compelled to holler:

'*Il est Champion du Monde!*'

Adam, Paul, Arthur, Ian, Jacqui, Valerie and Bianca all stared at me. But Stefan, the lanky bespectacled waiter, was looking at Arthur.

'*Champion du Monde*?!' Stefan was clearly impressed, although frankly, Arthur could probably have been a world champion vegetable grower and still have produced the same response. 'What is he champion of?'

Now I knew this one. I'd heard Luc say it loads of times this afternoon. Somehow I recalled '*soulever avec puissance*' correctly, and as I watched Stefan's proud French eyes light up, I suddenly realised the value of listening in class. I made a vow right then to become fluent in at least one other language as soon as I returned to England. (Then, four days later, I made a vow to forget it.)

Stefan shook Arthur's mighty hand vigorously, then ran off to tell the rest of the kitchen staff. Silence descended as shovelling commenced, but I didn't take the hint. Ian's meal was thus ruined by my insistence on resuming our interview.

'It's strange isn't it,' I said, 'that no one has ever done this sort of thing here before. You'd think, with all the great missionaries and evangelists there have been, that someone would have done it.'

'I believe that the devil has holds on certain places and areas' replied Ian, rather mysteriously. I hadn't expected Satan to enter this polite dinner-time conversation, but I was fascinated now.

'The devil?'

'Well, the forces of darkness at least. If you look in the Bible, when Jesus pulls those demons out of the man called Legion, they don't want to leave that particular area, even if they have to leave that man's body. So for me it seems biblical that spirits can have holds on towns and areas.'

'Are you saying that Châtel is possessed by the devil?'
He didn't answer.

'Now in some areas – especially in the inner cities – life is suppressed and everybody seems down. Well in an area like this one, Châtel, everything seems lovely – people have beautiful homes, they live in a beautiful landscape, they've got plenty of time, they're very friendly and upbeat. . . . After all, they spend their days skiing, eating cheese and drinking wine! But ultimately, there's a rejection of God's son here, and the message just hasn't been told to them. My feeling is that the devil likes to hold people in that place. You're more likely to call out to God in a place of desperation. So we often think that the hardest places to go are the prisons and the rough areas in the inner cities, but quite often those people are open to the gospel. But here people are being deceived – held in this place where everything is fine – and it's a spiritual hold. And to break through that is a very difficult thing, because without the drug dealers and the fights on every corner, everything seems on the surface to be fine. The hold doesn't appear as a visible thing – people aren't selling drugs and lagging drunk and using prostitutes – but there is a spiritual hold which blocks the eyes and ears from the truth of the Gospel.'

Ian was momentarily distracted by the excited collection of chefs and waiters who were craning out of the kitchen, whispering 'Champion du Monde!' Arthur's meal wasn't free, unfortunately, although at this point of the evening, his hopes were beginning to rise.

'So you think it's more difficult to come to a quiet, peaceful, relaxed place like this, than to walk into a violent city famed for violence and drugs?'

Quite by accident I provoked Ian into profoundly summing up the whole shebang:

'One place is very different from another. But this is the simple truth that we take everywhere we go; it's what drives us on and what saved us in the first place. Everyone, whoever they are and wherever they come from, needs Jesus Christ in their life.'

We had, as Enid Blyton might say, many more fantastic adventures that weekend. We hit the pavement pulpit again on the Sunday, we enjoyed fattening French food, and we watched *Match of the Day* on Lloyd's satellite TV. Fourteen more hours were well spent as we sang and joked our way back across the channel, and we even stayed in a robot hotel near Calais. But nothing we did for the rest of that weekend could demonstrate more clearly why we were there than Ian had, back in that restaurant. Tough Talk exists because its members have experienced the power of God first hand. Now they'll stop at nothing to tell the whole world about it.

Chapter 4

The Ballad Of Bob Spzalek

'Come on!'
  'Three white lights!'
  'Yes!'

Surely there must be some mistake? It's Saturday afternoon, and I'm sitting in the crowd at the British
Powerlifting Championships, in the middle of a very
serious gym in a suburb of Birmingham. This can't be
right . . .

I was, despite desperate pleas from my brain, in exactly
the right place. In the space of a few short months, I had
become so entangled with Tough Talk, Arthur and
powerlifting that objective journalism was now an
impossibility. They'd become my friends – an extended
family even – and it was for that very reason that I was
now sitting there on a broken wooden seat, supporting
Arthur in his quest for an eighth British title. I'd even
dragged a bunch of friends along with me to see it: the
now Arthur-addicted Little Phil, and our respective glut-
ton-for-punishment girlfriends. Nobody could tell us we
didn't know how to show women a good time!

If you've never paid a visit to the British Powerlifting Championships – and I'll assume of course that the vast majority of the world's population has – a few words of description may be helpful. Its purpose is fairly self-explanatory: to raise a champion from the British lifting scene, through the process of a thoroughly examining competition. Each entrant takes part in all three of the powerlifting disciplines (a quick reminder for those who need it – that's the squat, the bench-press and the dead-lift), performs three lifts in each category, takes the best (heaviest) lift from each, adds the total weight lifted together, and then hopes to have hoisted up more than anyone else. Put simply, the competitor who manages to lift the biggest total amount of weight over the three events is crowned champion.

Three judges encircle each pretender to the throne, scrutinising every movement to ensure that the lifts comply with the strict legalities of the competition rules. After each attempt, they then decide whether the lift was legal or not – creating the spectator-friendly element of the sport. On the stage, next to the lifting area, are six light bulbs, set out in two parallel rows of three. The top row of bulbs are clear, and so emit white light when they are switched on; the bottom row are coloured orange and therefore look like they've been stolen from nearby road-works. Each judge controls one white light – indicating a good lift – and one orange light – indicating a bad lift – via two buttons in his hand. Thus, after each elevation is completed, there's an agonising moment of tension as competitor and crowd all wait for the judges' decision to materialise.

For the 2002 championships, this all took place in the centre of a very large, very heavy-duty gymnasium, which bore more than a passing resemblance to the hall of an under-funded school. With its white no-nonsense walls and tall, girdered, manly roof, the agreeably-titled Tyseley Health and Fitness Centre seemed the perfect host for such a testosterone-pumping display of brute strength. Accessed from a route which led up iron stairs, through a cargo-bay tunnel lined with the wrecks of assorted motor vehicles, and past a row of photographs from particularly colourful boxing matches, it was hardly located on life's high street. No, this was a serious place, for serious people.

So excited was I by the prospect of this particularly repetitive and eyelid-straining day in the UK's sporting calendar, that I forced my party to turn up a full two hours early for Arthur's competition. That meant that, for our perusal and entertainment, the luscious ladies of local lifting would be gracing the platform in front of us first.

When the women's competition was announced by Ralph, the gentle giant in possession of the public address microphone, the platform in my head was graced by a collection of beasts from beyond. I pictured distorted, strained features. I imagined hideously overbuilt bodies, laden with muscles on muscles and resembling a badly misshapen balloon animal. I remembered the story about the woman with the beard. This was surely not going to be pretty . . . But for some reason, the anticipated gaggle of pigs-in-wigs never appeared. Instead, a string of very ordinary-looking women filtered out, one by one, looking like the nurses, schoolteachers, and supermarket-housewives that they probably were. In turn, each woman jacked up the kind of weights that I'd fail to move even if my life depended on it. And so preconception floated out of the window, closely pursued by pride.

The cream of the British powerlifting community had clearly gathered for the occasion. Dotted around the room were a number of bulky men in tight-fitting 'Great Britain Team' shell-suit jackets, a group of studious-looking officials in uncomfortable blazers with official-looking pocket patches, and a load of coaches and personal trainers, all of whom were doing their best to look important and involved. At the back of the hall, just next to the woman selling home-made sandwiches and rolls, there was even a drugs-testing unit, containing a tall, scrawny man (evidently a doctor, whom Arthur would be very pleased to urinate for later) who looked even more out of place than the tubby journalist. In fact, if only there'd been a few cameras from one of the more obscure satellite TV channels, and a few hundred more people in the friends-and-families crowd, then this might have been a heck of a show.

Almost two and a half hours after it had been scheduled to start, the men's competition was finally upon us. Previously preferring to hide his bulk in a sloppy sweatshirt, Arthur now revealed all in a tight-fitting black T-shirt, embroidered on either sleeve with bold white quotations from the Bible. One bicep read 'To God be the glory', while the other proclaimed 'The Lord is my strength.' Smiling nervously and wrapped up in Scripture, he grabbed James, his coach and son, and trudged through into the competitor's waiting area. The next time we would see him, he'd be attempting to squat for the first time all year.

I didn't quite understand the tactical planning involved in Arthur's pre-tournament training regime, even when he explained it to me beforehand:

'I haven't squatted at all for months now,' he'd confessed. 'I'm not really supposed to do it.'

'What about the bench-press?' I'd asked, spotting a potentially gaping hole in his chances.

'No, I haven't done any of that either. Oh – I tell a lie – I did one last week.'

'Any good?'

'No, not really. It's always been my weakest event.'

'And the other one? The deadlift?'

'Well, I do that all the time with Tough Talk don't I?'

So it seemed to me that Arthur was going to attempt to win the British title, over three events, after only training in one discipline. This sounded a bit like trying to win the triple jump when you've forgotten how to hop and skip. In an attempt at reassurance, I gave him a hollow tap on the shoulder, and explained how I thought he'd be fine. Then I spent a few moments trying hard to dislodge my tongue from my cheek.

On the stage, the vast men stepped up in order like a slow, but steady procession of giant children ready for a stint on some unfortunate Santa's knee. As four sturdy assistants stood close by, prepared for a heavy catch at the first sound of breaking bone, each of Arthur's rivals made their first squats look easy. Some shouted, some stared into space, some screamed and pulled a face. But everybody lifted, and lifted well. Everybody got three white lights. So when we heard that the next squat would be performed by our suddenly pale friend in the tight-fitting Bible-bashing outfit, the stakes suddenly got higher. It was only the first lift, and in a sense it didn't matter much. But everyone else had managed it – the stage was surely set for someone to fail. And it made me think – what if Arthur had gambled wrong? What if, in order to contend a major sporting honour, you do actually have to train beforehand? In a hazy moment of adrenaline and palm moisture, I realised that I had inherited my mother's blood pressure problem. And I realised just how much I suddenly cared about powerlifting. I grabbed for my girlfriend's hand. I got Little Phil's instead. It didn't matter. I squeezed twice as hard.

And then, just like at the prayer meeting a couple of months beforehand, there was a loud supernatural moment that nothing could have prepared me for. The stride was confident. The voice was loud:

'Wa-si-ma-kala-ta'

Arthur's volume control tugged sharply clockwise, muting the rest of us. And again:

'Oot-wa-si-kakaka-la-si'

Arthur was praying in tongues on the platform at the British powerlifting championships. And as I pondered whether he was doing it in order to call on strength from above, or to scare the Lycra pants off the opposition, he made the squat, no problem. Three white lights. A congratulatory shout from Ralph on the microphone. And a loud self-motivating 'Come on' from Arthur.

When Arthur shouts 'Come on', it's not aggressive. It's not intrusive either, or even laced with desperation. 'Come on' – an encouragement – to himself, to the spectators, to the other lifters. 'Come on' – as in, it's only a sport, it's the taking part that counts. 'Come on' – as if to say: well done son, well tried. . . . So as he stands to the side of the stage, and watches the next squat, he's saying it again: that same confident, friendly encouragement. Those two words tell us all that Arthur is a genuine sportsman: that he can see past rivalry and call the other lifters his friends. But they also tell us a lot more. They tell us, just as his pre-tournament preparations did, that the line between competition and demonstration has become blurred. After his initial tensions Arthur relaxed, returning not to the familiar state of the hardened and focused athlete, like those around him, but to that of the performer, the showman . . . even the evangelist. So as he stepped up for his second squat, he began to play the

crowd, to chat to the human safety nets fielding around
the bar, appearing at every moment as if he was getting
ready to shout 'and I believe I'm a bigger man thanks to
Jesus than I ever was before.'

The second lift passed as effortlessly as the first. A
quick burst of international prayer, one well-oiled movement and another 'Come on.' But as Arthur strode away
again, trying hard to suppress a little grin, another figure
lumbered into view. A huge, bald monster, with a thick
black goatee and two sets of shoulders. This, according to
Arthur's wife Jacqui, who'd sidled up next to me, was
Bob Spzalek, favourite for the competition amongst
those in the know, and long-time arch-rival of our hero.

Of course, I can clearly understand now, with most of the
adrenaline drained from my veins, that Bob Spzalek is
almost certainly a very nice man indeed. He's probably a
heck of a bloke: the kind who'll always help an old lady
across the road, or stop and help if ever he spots a damsel
in distress. However, for the purposes of the next hour and
a half, he had become the enemy. He and Arthur were
swiftly polarised by my overactive imagination –
Whitebeard versus Blackbeard; good versus evil; England
versus Germany. By the time he'd got his hands on the bar,
he was playing the bad guy in the action movie in my head.

'Three white lights!' Ralph announced cheerily.

Hearts sank in the White camp. Spzalek had just
squatted the same amount of weight as Arthur, putting
them thick neck to thick neck. He was living up to form.
Looking distinctly like an American wrestler, he strolled
back past Whitebeard and son, resisting the chance to
waste a good eyeballing too early on. He'd whacked the
ball right back to the other end of the court.

'Arthur White, 277.5 kilos.' Ralph's announcement
seemed to come around too quickly. It was his turn again
already – it was up to him now to raise the stakes further.

Our man had squatted only twice this year. Both of those very successful attempts had taken place in the last twenty minutes. Surely he couldn't keep going on like this? Had my PE teacher been lying to me through all those cruel lessons? Is practice completely irrelevant?

Arthur's confident swagger was now in full swing. He kept, almost involuntarily, raising his thumb in our general direction, and his communications with the judges were turning into nods and winks. As he approached the now heavily loaded bar, he smiled at each of the safety men, and declined their help when getting into position. From the wings of the platform, Spzalek looked on with a nervous grimace. Enthused, we stood to our feet, ready for another fine moment of odds-defying power. But it didn't arrive. Instead, Arthur was caught off-guard by the jump in weight, and, after squatting to the floor, bar-on-shoulders, he found himself struck by a momentary paralysis. He couldn't get the bar back up again. A quiet 'no' trickled from his lips, and eight unwelcome hands hammocked the weight. Three orange lights. Disaster.

Spzalek ordered his facial muscles to attention. Not a speck of emotion crossed his shiny face. But he could smell a chance here, as Arthur found his way back to base, unable to apply the same emotional restraint. Ten strong steps later, he was looking at the same bar that had just defeated his oponent. No prayers left his lips; no self-motivating shout echoed around the now-silent hall. Instead, there was simply focus. His locked stare flinched slightly as he took the weight on his shoulders. His bald pink head began to redden as he sank into the squat. Then, as his perfect vertical ascent led to the inevitable triple-barrelled burst of white light, the tiniest fleck of positivity began to seep from the corners of his mouth. He'd done it. And now the emotion came – like a tidal wave full of leaping salmon. Suddenly the craggy features came to life, and in the midst of a scream of self-congratulation, the frightened air took a bodyswerve as Spzalek's heavy fist whooshed through it. Ten steps had taken him out to the lift – five bounding strides saw him back. Now he looked at Arthur, now the eyeballs were raging. A little shell-shocked, and rocked by the realisation that his non-attendance at the gym was now paying the wrong kind of dividends, his rival simply gazed at his failing hands.

A fifteen-minute break provided welcome punctuation. Arthur beckoned me across as we waited, the wind a little removed from his previously pumped sails. It was time that he explained something to me.

'Listen son' he said, in the manner of a father welcoming a child to sit on his outstretched knee. 'I don't want you to think that I've not been training because I'm lazy.'

'I didn't think that,' I lied.

'Well it's fine if you did. But it's not true. The truth is that I shouldn't really be squatting at all. Ever. You see, when the drugs were at their worst, and I was lifting the most, I really didn't care about my body. I didn't care what happened to it – I just wanted to be World Champion, again and again. But the more I lifted, and the more drugs I took, the more damage I was doing to myself, and particularly to my legs. A few years ago I ended up having operations to repair both of them – they were both severely bowed and buckled. The surgeon cut both my legs in half, and then put them back together. He said I'd be lucky if I could walk again. So as you can imagine, I shouldn't really be here, doing this.'

(Later I discovered that one of Steve Johnson's favourite jokes is 'Arthur had to have his legs cut in half – he was seven foot three when I first met him.')

'So why do you put your body in danger like this?' I couldn't help but ask. 'Why didn't you give up lifting there and then, and take up snooker?'

Arthur looked down at his embroidered sleeve.

'The Lord is my strength,' he said, with real pride.

The bench-press may sound like the most inviting of the three disciplines – instead of standing up to lift muscle-bursting weights you at least get the opportunity to lie down and do it – but it's arguably the hardest of the lot. I remember having a go at forty kilos of it in Châtel, and feeling rather hurt when, having screamed 'no more', I was informed that I hadn't actually taken the strain yet. To be any good you need to develop a whole new set of muscles in the backs of the arms, instead of just using the 'brute strength' that we've all got hidden away somewhere. Put simply, it's hard, and it hurts.

Clearly, this wasn't Arthur's forte either. He opened at a light weight, just to make sure of registering at least one good lift. Spzalek immediately went in higher. Both succeeded, meaning that Spzalek was now racing clear. Arthur lifted again; Spzalek raised him again – this time by double the margin. Six white lights and two Ralph-shouts later, the enemy was over fifty kilos ahead.

Arthur thought long and hard about his cards. He still had the ace – his Tough Talk-groomed deadlift, to pull out on the home straight. He reckoned that he could pull back fifty kilos on anyone. That meant he just needed to keep up for now. He made his hare-and-tortoise philosophy known to coach James, who passed on the information to Ralph. So again, Arthur attempted an increased weight that he knew was within him. Three white lights, three good lifts.

But Spzalek wasn't intent on playing the game. Seeing Arthur's limited success, and knowing from past experience that he needed a healthy lead before the dead-lift, he decided to put plenty of clear blue water between them. If he made it, Arthur would probably need a World Record deadlift to win the title.

But he didn't make it. Instead, in a reversal of his emotions after the final squat, Spzalek became a picture of disappointment. The giant head shook. Failing fist punched failing palm. Spzalek, like Macbeth before him, had overreached. And after Arthur's moderate accomplishment, he knew that there was less than forty kilos between them, going into the final round. In a way it was a shame that the TV cameras had never turned up: they were missing a treat.

At this point it should be explained that Arthur was on a very tight schedule here. Tough Talk were due on stage at 8.34 p.m., 100 miles north, in Manchester, where 3,000 young people were expected to pack the Apollo Theatre, and the god-fearing, weight-lifting, story-telling Tough Talk show had top billing. Ian, Steve and Marcus were already there, waiting for Arthur to finish his competition and join them. Only trouble was, with the deadlift still to come, it was already pushing 6.30 p.m.

This troubled Arthur. Generally, Tough Talks don't happen without him. It's a pretty set pattern – Arthur speaks at the start, then Arthur lifts near the end – and whilst the team were open to experimentation in smaller venues, now was perhaps not the time. He knew that if he left at that moment, he'd have a chance of making it through the post-football traffic. Was he being greedy by finishing the job? Or selfish? As the next stage of the competition started to gear up, and Ralph attempted to breathe new life into the tired crowd (who, considering the time, were now in severe danger of missing *Blind Date*), Arthur spotted his wife Jacqui, and sought her counsel.

The draw had been kind to Arthur. Spzalek was due to lift first, meaning that World Record or not, the possibility of victory was at least in Arthur's own battered hands. So far he'd lifted a total of 400 kilos, with Spzalek just ahead on 432.5. Unless his rival had a truly great lift hidden up his sleeve, glory was in sight.

Both men posted their opening bids with the stone-faced officials. On the first lift alone, Arthur was attempting to make up more than half of the 32-kilo deficit. He managed it without much difficulty, which caused obvious concern in the Spzalek camp. So with Arthur winning the contest of strength, it seemed an appropriate moment for Spzalek to start playing mind games.

'Bob Spzalek' announced Ralph, as we geared up for round eight of Rumble in the Brum-hall.

The silence boomed, as if greeting a joke of the poorest quality.

'Bob Spzalek?'

Suddenly the audience was shaken from its slumber. Where was the moustachioed master?

'I have to remind you that you have one minute to reach the platform. Otherwise your lift will be forfeited.' Ralph clearly had no more idea about what was going on than the rest of us. 'Ten seconds . . . five . . . four . . . three . . . two . . . one . . . '

The three orange lights flashed on and off. Still there was no sign of Spzalek. Whatever the reason for his no-show, it placed Arthur firmly in the driving seat. Confident, but confused, Arthur stepped up for the lift that would place him a slender 7.5 kilos ahead. But just before stooping for the bar, he paused. Something was wrong. Suddenly the palms were hot, the eyes were darting, and the brow was furrowed. Had he been successfully psyched-out by Spzalek? Or was his mind on Manchester, a hundred miles and surely more than ninety minutes away? Yes, that was surely it – as he stood on the doorstep of a sixth British title, he was questioning himself: wondering whether he should be lifting here at all, in front of a hundred or so of his friends and enemies, and not in front of 3,000 wide-eyed kids. The judge to his left coughed with impatience. Arthur looked up despairingly, tormented by his inner conflict. But on raising that head he saw Jacqui, beaming back at him with those 'through-thick-and-thin' eyes. The left hand gripped the bar. Habitually, the right one followed. One massive exertion of power and strength, and one almighty 'Come on!'

Three white lights. Arthur White was in the lead.

* * *

Meanwhile, backstage in Manchester, the organiser of the youth event, Andy Hawthorne, was getting a little flustered. Tough Talk were due to play a supporting role to a well-known Christian band called The Tribe, and as that group timed dance moves and light changes to the split second, Hawthorne was a little perturbed to see Ian, Steve and Marcus kicking their heels and reading the newspaper.

'Shouldn't you lads be rehearsing or something?' he asked, pacing and fidgeting as the important hour approached.

'Well, we don't normally do rehearsals,' replied Ian, a little taken aback. He looked across at the troupe of performers, as they went through their choreographed motions for the hundredth time. 'I mean, how can you rehearse squatting 500 pounds?'

'You don't rehearse. Right.' He gritted his teeth and looked heavenwards for help.

'We just sort of . . . go out there and . . . give it some. Know what I mean?'

This may have been a north–south thing, but no, Hawthorne didn't know what he meant. A large team of people had spent weeks putting this evening together. They'd ploughed bags of time, money, energy, prayer and love into it – hoping that for once, the Christians might be able to lay claim to the best party in town. Now this stage-cluttering band of undignified, unshaven, unrehearsed lumps – one of whom hadn't even had the decency to turn up yet – were standing poised to ruin the whole thing. The organiser trudged slowly away, shaking his head, and Ian grinned sheepishly. Where on earth was Arthur?

* * *

Arthur was still in Birmingham, chewing on his own heart. Spzalek had re-emerged, and had informed the officials of his intention to attempt a massively increased weight. There was still no reason given for his mysterious disappearance a few minutes earlier, but speculating onlookers reckoned he was conserving his energy for this final odds-defying lift. Anyhow, whatever was going on inside Spzalek's polished head, success now would leave Arthur needing a World Record to win the title.

'Bob Spzalek,' called Ralph, uncertainly.

Suddenly there was hush once more. Emitting a low growl, the giant man plodded deliberately towards the platform. He looked down at the well-stocked metal bar – this was far more than he'd usually lift. Placing one titanic foot into position, then another, he began the mental prep-work. Five seconds of excruciating, back-breaking, life-shortening pain would almost certainly bring him victory over his old enemy. He stroked a shimmering bicep. A quick glance at the scoreboard behind him confirmed the total scores: White 690 kilos,

Spzalek 682.5 kilos. Three white lights would equal a 25-kilo lead.

The crowd could bear silence no longer. A shout of 'Come on Dad' punctured the peace, and the floodgates swung open. Spzalek's many friends and supporters began to clap, cheer and chant. Arthur looked nervously at his son. This was the moment, and didn't we know it.

The grip tightened. Spzalek looked up. Slowly but surely the bar began its vertical ascent. In slow-motion the balanced hunk of metal made it up past the ankles, then the shins. Spzalek, spewing forth sweat and turning a terrifying beetroot, began to straighten his back. Almost there. The knees locked; the head rose up – another second and the lift would be complete. 'Drop it!' whispered Little Phil. But the final second passed – we looked up from behind our cower-shield hands and saw that he was still there. The neck pulsed; the fingers trembled; the sweat now gushed. But he'd done it . . . he'd taken the 25-kilo lead . . . the competition was his . . .

And then it wasn't. Literally, the whole thing just slipped through his fingers. Time froze as we realised what had happened – the grip had given way at the last, decisive moment. Then time unfroze, and the colossal weight came crashing down on the unsuspecting floor. Three orange lights. Spzalek: utterly cast down. And Arthur White was British Powerlifting Champion.

In the corner of the gym, Arthur hugged his son and sincerely thanked the heavens. Then, in a move that was clearly pre-meditated, he made an unexpected announcement that would whip up the crowd into an even greater frenzy. With the competition won and one lift to go, he was going for the World Record.

And then Arthur the powerlifter disappeared, and his replacement – the confident crowd-pleaser from Tough Talk – bowled into the fray. 'Come on!' he shouted, clapping his hands rhythmically above his head. 'Come on!' He gave the wounded Spzalek a consolatory high-five. Every competitor was cheering; all onlookers were on their feet. Then, as he gripped the bar proudly, as if it was a trophy itself, the chanting began: 'Arthur, Arthur, Arthur . . . '

The bar barely made it past his knees, but the attempt provided us all with enough adrenaline to make the drive home safe. He shook his head and smiled. There'd be other World Record attempts. But, as he realised, gazing at his latest eyesore trophy, there might not be another chance to tell 3,000 children his story. The clock didn't lie. We had little more than an hour to travel a hundred unknown miles. The drugs test, the change of clothes and the 'hard-luck-Bob-close-one-this-year' were all over in seconds. Then we were chasing Arthur out of the gym and towards the car park.

* * *

It's hard to put a finger on, but I think the exact moment we realised that we weren't going to make it was when we arrived in Liverpool, at least thirty miles west of our intended destination. So when we finally reached the Apollo Manchester, just as 3,000 young people were attempting to swamp the exits, Arthur was fully expecting a red-faced barrage of anger from Ian McDowall. Instead, he got a hug and an impromptu round of applause. And while Arthur poured out his feelings of shame for not getting there in time, I realised what an enormous venue this was. They'd gone from a poky school to a giant theatre in just a few months. At this rate, Tough Talk would be doing the stadium tour in 2004.

'You should have seen it!' enthused Ian, his face alive with excitement.

'I'm so sorry,' Arthur replied, almost tearful. 'I shouldn't have competed today. I should have been here.'

Ian simply smiled, before being surprised by a hug from the relieved Andy Hawthorne. The organiser muttered words like 'fantastic' and 'unbelievable', then wandered away again in what appeared to be a state of excited shock.

'It doesn't matter Arthur. We had an incredible night here tonight. We made a challenge at the end of the night and about two hundred kids came forward. They reckon that's the best response they've ever had at one of these events.' Behind him, Andy Hawthorne was still grinning.

Arthur gripped his shiny plastic trophy tightly. He'd barely had time to realise that he'd won the British Championships for the sixth time.

'I wanted to show them,' he stumbled. 'I wanted to show them that I won it drug-free.'

Ian put a reassuring arm around his shoulder, and we headed toward the eager posse of young and misguided autograph-hunters. And as the reunited team stood with pens in hand, I realised that we'd all learned an important lesson. Tough Talk is not about Arthur White, or indeed about any one man. It's about a story written by God Himself, and a show that may be loud, powerful and exciting, but where ultimately, He is pulling the strings.

Two hundred lives changed, and the British title in the bag. Not bad for a day's work.

* * *

As we made our way back to London the following afternoon, I found myself struck by an unexpected bout of objectivity. With the trip to New York less than a week away, I'd already completed three legs of my Tough Talk tour – three sides in fact, of the planned trapezium. The London school, the streets of France, and the mission to Manchester were all behind me now. It'd all been great fun, but it seemed that something important was still missing from the story. In London I'd seen children struck dumb by the power of Steve's story. In Châtel we may well have done something significant on a supernatural level. And now in Manchester, 200 people 'allegedly' made the decision to become Christians. But in all that time, after all that Bible-bashing, the journalist travelling with Tough Talk had never actually seen a single person committing this oft-mentioned act of 'giving one's life.' Because even in Manchester, I'd missed the boat and heard it all second hand. So now, in this moment of doubt and weakness, I allowed myself a moment to wonder if all this was quite as 'exciting' and 'phenomenal' as I'd first thought. Were Tough Talk the dynamic team of evangelists I'd been led to believe they were? Or were they as good at telling stories as they were at lifting weights?

I made a secret pact with myself. I'd give them one more week to really amaze me. The mind stayed open. A giant Boeing 747 hovered overhead, and I began to count the hours.

Chapter 5

Lifting Off

Suddenly, the plane lurches sideways, then tilts as if King Kong has just aimed a right hook at its defenceless wing. Lights flash, hostesses panic, children scream. That Hollywood moment with the falling oxygen masks plays right before my eyes in 3-D, Widescreen and Glorious Technicolor. My stomach is doing somersaults . . . looks like a couple of the engines are too. This really doesn't look too good. *I think we're going to crash.*

The frantic muffled Tannoy tells us to assume the crash position – heads between knees kissing backsides goodbye. In defiance, three seatbelts unclip. Taking careful grips on the spinning cabin, Arthur White, Ian McDowall and Steve Johnson stagger out of their seats and into the aisle.

'It might look as if we're in trouble,' splutters Ian, his face drained of colour, as he reaches the front of the passenger section, 'but if you listen to us, you'll be OK.'

'We're a group of Christians,' continues Arthur to all who'll listen. 'We used to be criminals, drug addicts and violent hardmen, but an encounter with Jesus Christ saved us. Our lives have been powerfully changed, and it's not too late for yours to be changed too.'

The plane is diving, shaking and dancing in the sky. The clouds are above us, then below us. The raging Atlantic plays the same game. Lights flicker on and off, baggage bursts forth from dented lockers. But the people are silent, focused on the three extraordinary men whom this tempest is tossing around the canister like worms. Battered, bruised and bloody, not for the first time in his life, Steve finds a way to his feet and addresses the horrified rollercoaster-riders before him:

'2,000 years ago, God sent His son to die so that you lot might live on forever, even after death. And all you have to do is acknowledge Him. You just have to pray; you just have to tell Him that you're sorry for the mistakes you've made, and the things you've done against Him.'

A tumultuous crack sounds around the aircraft, and Steve is launched towards the rear, knocking himself out cold in a swift encounter with the lavatory. Undeterred, Ian and Arthur grip tighter, look quickly at one another, and continue their Last Supper sermon.

'Jesus Christ will save you from anything you face now,' shouts Arthur. 'With Him you have nothing to fear – not even death. So I ask you a question: who would like to pray with us now?'

Every hand in the cabin thrusts upwards. So does the plane, and an overhead baggage cabinet takes care of Arthur. Ian looks down briefly at his two unconscious companions (still sliding noisily around the floor), closes his eyes and prays out loud. Every pair of eyes closes, bar those peeping from my quivering face. I'm staring out of the window, watching the ocean race towards us like a giant blue portrait of death himself. And suddenly Ian stops praying and falls to his knees, and the lights flicker off for a final time. The torrent of spins and loops settles down into a simple nosedive, and the peace of God sucks every scream from every mouth. We plummet

towards our final destination in silence – in a beautiful,
deathly silence.

I wake up suddenly, with a cold layer of sweat forming a
harsh wet sponge on my back.

'Are you alright?' asks Adam McMillan, prodding my
wrinkled forehead with the lithe fingers of a one-time
thief.

I take a moment to establish my surroundings. It looks
as if I'm still on the plane from London, and that *Vanilla
Sky*, which sent me to sleep in the first place, has now finished.

'Yeah, I'm fine. Just don't like flying very much.'

I'm no dream analyst, and I'm certainly no great believer
in people who actually earn money from telling you that
a dream about your dog is actually a reference to your
past life as Cleopatra's manservant, but it occurred to me
that the fictional plane crash episode might have meaning. I'm terrified of flying, after a particularly bumpy
ride to Turkey a few years back, so that would appear to
make the plane crash part of the dream fairly self-
explanatory (provided the theory that fish, mice and
canaries have cat-nightmares holds with you). But this
wasn't just a disaster movie, taking up from where the
disastrous *Vanilla Sky* had left off. This was a short story
about salvation: about a brief enforced pilgrimage across
35,000 vertical feet. And the bittersweet ending – a complicated double helix of death and life – had a generally
upbeat feel to it.

In my dream, the Tough Talkers chose to fulfil their
calling to the final second. Even faced with impending
death, they showed no fear or weakness. Instead, they
surveyed their final crowd (a captive audience, it must be
said), and launched into a final presentation of their

beliefs. So after the laid-back experience of Châtel, and the snapshot of the London school where I first saw them work, I'd been subconsciously convinced that these people were of a certain calibre. This is how I now saw Tough Talk: as a group of men so shaken by the miraculous transformations in their lives, that they'll stop at nothing to tell others of the good news they'd discovered. As the Blues Brothers would say, they're on a mission from God.

* * *

Of course, sitting on a plane to New York in 2002 can never be a wholly relaxing experience, considering the epoch-defining scenes of the previous September, the memories of which still loom large over that city and all who visit her. September 11th 2001 was the day that a plane became a weapon, so when a passenger boards now, we're forced to wonder – if only for an instant – whether this flight could be the next to end in engineered tragedy. I remember, as we all do, where I was when I watched the tumultuous events of that day unfold – I was standing, rooted to the spot, with a clutch of other journalists in the newsroom at Premier Radio. Julia Fisher was there, so was Little Phil. In silence we all stood there – with our jaws open, our heads shaking and our eyes overcome with saltiness. I remember the whole thing very clearly – it stabbed at me like it stabbed at every Western heart. Literally it was 'the day that changed the world,' but in the worst possible circumstances. Weeks later I'd managed to flush most of the library footage out of the 'repeat play' section in my mind, but one thought remained. I couldn't help wondering about the people on the aircraft – the people who had expected to make a quick, safe trip across the country for business, or to see family, or just to get away for a few days. What went through their minds – knowing what was going to happen minutes before we did? How did they cope, staring death in the face like that?

So now, I can't help fearing that I might be on the next tube of victims to be turned into a missile. For that reason I buckled myself in tightly on this, my first flight since that terrorist outrage.

Also, due to the revelations over who was responsible, there's now an unfortunate racial issue in the air. Men and women of Arabic appearance are now more likely to be searched, questioned and even turned away from flights these days. Any law-abiding businessman, shopkeeper, student or doctor who happens to have been born in a certain part of the world, or descend from people who were, is now made to shift uneasily in their seat for the duration of the flight by two hundred pairs of suspicious eyes, all owned by would-be vigilantes ready to leap on them if they so much as get up to visit the lavatory. So flying has changed, for all of us just like the world has, and for the same reason.

* * *

Three hours after leaving Heathrow, the adrenaline rush from discovering our free toothbrushes and socks was beginning to wear off. In an attempt to pass a little time, and ward away the threat of deep-vein thrombosis, Adam and I decided to take a short stroll around the plane. Obviously there wasn't too much to see, and so after making our third swift circuit, we were beginning to earn concerned looks from some of the cabin crew. One of them, a pretty blonde hostess in her twenties, made a beeline for the more thuggish-looking Adam.

Arthur White doing a one-handed deadlift

World Championships, Canada 2001 – Gold Medal Deadlift 750lb

The team in France with author Martin Saunders
in front

Adam and Paul encourage a youngster from the crowd
in Chatel, France, April 2002

**Arthur collecting the British Champion
award**

**Street outreach Tough Talk style, with locals looking
on – Queens, New York**

Steve Johnson shares his story in Queens, New York

An excited crowd in New York

Team talk before evening meeting at Christ's Tabernacle, New York

Getting the pastors involved. Adam Durse, of Christ's Tabernacle, New York, joins in with the fun

The cross at Ground Zero,
New York

Clearance work at Ground Zero,
New York

**The Tough Talk team being encouraged by the
Archbishop of Canterbury at CRE**

**Arthur collecting 'Evangelist Extraordinaire'
award**

'Can I help you at all?' she asked him, over-smiling as all hostesses must.

'Nah, thanks,' came the gruff reply. 'We're just having a walk around.'

She clearly wasn't satisfied. Adam is not a large man – in fact, he's small enough to find himself the butt of three or four size jokes an hour from Steve – but he is well put-together, and thus merited a little further suspicion. She tried again:

'You're with that party over there aren't you?' she nodded towards the area of the plane where Tough Talk were causing a weight imbalance. 'Where are you all going?'

'We're a group of Christians,' he explained off pat. 'We go around telling people how our lives were changed.'

'Oh right.' She was unfazed, but paused, before: 'And how was that then?'

'I'm sorry?'

'How were they changed?'

This caught both of us slightly off guard. Air hostesses, like hairdressers, taxi drivers and certain members of the Samaritans, are the kings and queens of polite conversation. As a rule, their true interest levels in what you say to them are remarkably low. It's a game – they ask a question, you answer, but really all they're thinking about is the road, or your hair, or how there's smoke coming out of the engine. But this girl is different. She's actually interested in people. Or at least, she's intrigued as to why a large group of big men who look about as Christian as Osama bin Laden, are travelling halfway across the world to tell their life stories.

'Well . . . ' starts Adam, 'we all used to be pretty bad people. We all come from the East End of London, and we were all involved, in one way or another, with a few things that we shouldn't have been.'

'Like what?'

'I was a thief. Arthur over there was a cocaine addict. Ian used to fight with knives and bats. Steve was a football hooligan . . . '

'Right. I see.' Thankfully she stops him before he gets on to Paul's eating habits. 'You were pretty bad weren't you?'

This isn't a fob off. She's still interested, which I find quite remarkable, considering that such tales of testosterone are usually better appreciated by gentlemen, not ladies.

'So what happened? What changed you?'

(This is what Christians like to call 'a golden opportunity.' This is like taking a penalty against a blind goalkeeper, or stealing a rattle from a sleeping child. From this point, it was almost impossible for Adam not to share his faith. In fact, one of the reasons that the British church is haemorrhaging so terribly is that the vast majority of Christians think that 'The Great Commission' – Jesus' command that His followers go out and spread the word – means sitting around and waiting for these magic moments to materialise.)

'We all believe that we met Jesus Christ – that he's a real person who we can still communicate with today. And through meeting Him, and having a relationship with Him, we changed.'

The hostess smiled, and puffed out her cheeks.

'Well I'm not sure what I believe about that. I think I believe in God, but . . . My boyfriend is a soldier, you see. He's out in Afghanistan right now. And all you can do is just pray, can't you? But how can you pray to a God you can't see? And how can you believe in a God who lets bad things happen – lets him go out there to fight in the first place?'

I found this all very strange. If she'd walked past a man in the street, waving a Bible and shouting out prophecies from the book of Revelation, I've no doubt that she would have walked on by. But bumping into Adam 'The Villain' McMillan made her pour out questions of life, death and eternity from the bottom of her heart. She looked him up and down, glanced back across at Ian, who was hugging his daughter with an over-developed bicep, and then said:

'You don't look much like a bunch of Christians, if you don't mind me saying so.' Which is what, obviously, she'd been thinking from the start. 'You look a lot more like a group of criminals.'

'Which is what we were,' beamed The Villain. 'But Jesus Christ changed us.'

For a moment she was lost in thought. In my head I hear the words that Arthur repeats every time he's got a microphone in his hands: 'you can believe what you like . . . but you cannot deny the truth of how our lives have changed.'

'Makes you think, doesn't it?' she said rhetorically to both and neither of us. Then, suddenly: 'Oh look, the seatbelt light has come on – we must be expecting a little turbulence. You'd better get back to your seats.'

And with that she ushered us back. But for the rest of the flight, she seemed a different, quieter, less artificial person. I don't know whether she was thinking about her army boyfriend, or the religious nuts she'd just encountered. But she was thinking, and ultimately that's the greatest reaction that any evangelist can hope for.

An hour – and one very palatable Chicken Tikka – later, the until-then lifeless young man on my right leapt without warning into conversational action. He was about my height, about my age, about my skin colour. He was wearing glasses; so was I. He had the Chicken Tikka too . . . and so on.

'Did you know that sixty-four people die every year on aircraft? Just from natural causes!'

'No,' I smiled, feigning at least a degree of interest. 'I didn't know that.'

'Apparently, they just cover them over with a blanket, and pretend that they're asleep, or ill. They have to put seatbelts on them too, so that when the plane lands, they don't fly forwards into the seat in front!'

As I've explained, I'm not too good with planes as it is. But by this point, five hours into a seven-hour flight, I'd come to terms with my hi-jacking and explosion-at-take-off fears. A new worry, concerning my sudden but improbable death through choking, heart attack or curry poisoning, I did not need. I smiled as he continued enthusiastically.

'The hostesses aren't allowed to let on, you see, in case it causes a panic. So they still bring them meals, and keep talking to them as if everything's normal. Then at the end of the flight they just zip 'em up in a mortuary bag. And you never know when it's going to happen – I mean, that bloke next to you . . . you think he's asleep . . . '

I looked across at Adam, who was once again away with the fairies.

'If I worried every time he had a nap, I'd have a heart condition by now.'

'Digby,' he said, with outstretched hand.

I introduced myself, and asked him where he was going. Then he asked the same of me, and we talked about what we'd be doing there. It was fun enough at the time, but not really worthy of immortalising on paper. So instead of the extended version, with all the speech marks and extra descriptive verbs and adjectives and things, I'll keep it brief.

Digby, 23, from London, was on his way to New York to visit friends, after giving up his job in IT recruitment.

He'd read philosophy at college, and as such was an evangelist's nightmare. He was very concerned by the way that the wing next to Adam's window was wobbling so violently, and wasn't sure whether he believed in God or not, although he added that he was 'not very interested in all that stuff.'

He was interested however in the whole Tough Talk story. He, like many others, had noticed at check-in that our group were all wearing the same blue bomber jackets, each one embroidered with an appropriately aggressive logo. He'd assumed that they all went to the same gym, or worked on the same TV chat show. He hadn't made any spiritual association, and so had been deceived into letting his guard down and asking the sixty-four thousand dollar 'What's Tough Talk?' question. As I explained, he listened very genuinely. Then he thought about it, just like the hostess (who was still thinking), and I wondered how a group of men with muscles could make such short work of the massive sacred/secular divide that cleaves through our culture.

* * *

There were sixteen of us on this flight. Marcus and his wife had jammed themselves a free upgrade to Upper Class because she worked for the airline. Ian's family reclined upstairs in first class, as his wife had demanded that she at least suffer her acute fear of flying in reasonable comfort. That left the other twelve disciples, me included, crammed into economy. On the negative side, this meant that I could tell what Adam had for breakfast. On the positive, it made twelve-way conversation a lot more straightforward. To my left snored Adam. A row in front, Steve and Ian sat reading intelligent spiritual reading matter (ten years ago they'd have been holding

Muscle and Fitness or *Playboy*). Behind me: Arthur and wife. On the other side of the aisle were Ian's pastor, Sean, and a new Tough Talk recruit, Gordon, who I was yet to meet properly. Also in the party were three people from Arthur's church, whose chief role on the trip was to pray for its success and our safety. Oh, and somewhere, Paul was asking if there was any more chocolate dessert.

'It's a strange place for missionaries to visit, isn't it?' I asked anybody who'd listen.

Ian turned, slightly puzzled.

'New York . . . well America even,' I continued. 'I mean, they practically invented evangelism over there didn't they? Billy Graham and all that.'

'We've been out there twice before,' Ian explained. 'We made some good friends in some of the churches, and I think maybe we made a difference to a few people's lives. But after the planes hit on September 11th, some of us felt a real bond with the people out there who were suffering, watching it all happen. And at that point we knew that we wanted to go back, to go out there again, if it was possible. And God made it possible, so here we are.'

'We stood at the bottom of the Twin Towers last time we came out,' said Adam, back from his coma (on my right, Digby sighed with relief, then continued to pretend he wasn't listening). 'I remember thinking then, just from a builder's point of view – there's no way in the world you could ever bring all that down. It just didn't seem possible.'

For a short time we were all quiet again, following those words through to their ground-shaking conclusion. The towers, the crash, the Pentagon, the failed fourth plane, the terrorists, the explosions, that tidal wave of debris: all that brain-etched BBC news footage was back from its slumber. The death, the destruction, the terrible waste of life: it all played out silently in our minds. So dark, so bleak – so hopeless.

'That's why we're going,' said Ian, firmly. 'Because the people out there need hope.'

'Did you hear about that whole office in the World Trade Center,' ventured Arthur from the seat behind mine, 'where they all became Christians just before the towers went down?'

I'd heard a lot of stories about the World Trade Center. Incredible stories of triumph over adversity; of accidental avoidance – sleeping through alarms, or just popping off for a coffee before work; of rescue and escape. But I didn't think I'd heard this one. I shook my head.

'It was an office above where the first plane hit. Seven hundred people were in there, and they were all left with no escape. They all knew they were almost certain to die – and they just had to sit there – waiting and screaming and going mad. There was this one guy who was a Christian and who got them all together to pray. He just explained that it wasn't too late for them to realise the reality of God – which of course was suddenly staring them all in the face. They all prayed together, and became Christians – seven hundred of them. Some of them even made phone calls to relatives to explain that "everything was going to be alright now".'

'Incredible,' I said, and meant it. 'Did they all die?'

'Every one. But they knew their fate already when they made those phone calls.'

Strange, I thought. I had a dream a bit like that.

* * *

'Bess' Wes'ern 'otel? Broa'way? Twenny minutes.'

I don't know what I expected America to be like, but it wasn't like this.

On arrival at Newark airport, we'd been ushered, packed and squeezed into two vehicles: a beaten-up grey minibus that had echoes of the A-Team van, and a glorious chunk of shiny red metal called Lincoln. I found myself in the latter, squashed even tighter than ever, between my now close friend Paul, and 'big' Steve Johnson, whom I didn't know at all, mainly due to the fact that he's the most terrifying-looking man I've ever sat next to. Now this was a big car – and at least a medium-sized one by American standards – but that's little help when you're being sandwiched between two champion pie-eaters. As I peeped into the evening air from a position in which I could barely breathe any, my brain and body began a five-day conversation about exactly what time it really was. Then, just as we were getting ourselves uncomfortable, a giant Hispanic man bounded into the car and gave the suspension a serious heart condition. With a thick smile illuminating his dark, hairy face, he turned to us, grinned, rammed his foot onto the accelerator, and began the speedy jolt towards New York City.

For a few moments we were all pale and silent, as the G-forces of the big man's driving pinned us to our seats in the same way that take-off had, hours earlier. In an attempt to be sociable, he turned to us (without slowing down, which only made us paler and quieter), and said something in extremely broken English. At this point, Steve wondered out loud whether we'd been kidnapped, and were on our way to Mexico. Paul and I exchanged glances of bewilderment, and said nothing. The driver tried again. Steve ventured an embarrassed, 'Yeah mate.' Then Sean O'Boyle, the leader of Ian's church who had been gaping out of the window at all the other big cars since first grabbing the front seat, broke his stare and attempted a full conversation. The driver said a hundred things. Sean turned and reported back that his name was Dario, and that he came from Puerto Rico. This impressed us greatly, and we congratulated him for his translation skills.

Dario the big Dominican decided that the best way to communicate to his ignorant new friends would be through the universal language of music. Looking at him as he flicked through his dashboard CD collection, we hypothesised that we'd soon be deafened by some Hip-Hop, amused by a Ricky Martin soundalike, or sexed-up by a bit of Swing. What we didn't expect was Celine Dion.

'This my favourite song – Titanic song' announced Dario proudly, before hitting the volume control and announcing it to the whole of New York state. And so began a musical adventure through every song that didn't seem to suit this car and this driver. UB40, Blondie – even George Michael had put in a 'Careless Whisper' by the time we'd finished. We sang along too, timidly at first, but when enthused by Dario's obvious excitement that we knew the words, with real gusto. By the time we'd reached our hotel, half an hour after his 'twenny minute' promise had expired, we'd taken a shine to old Dario, as he had to us. After he'd parked, he was approached by the intimidating figure of Arthur, whose bones had just been given a severe shake in the A-Team van.

'Hello mate,' said Arthur, as cheerily as his wobbly legs could allow.

''Ello,' came a reply uncommitted to comprehension.

'We'd like you to pick us up tomorrow lunchtime.'

'Yes.' He clearly didn't understand.

'Lunchtime? About twelve o'clock.'

'Twelve . . . o'clock?' The face spoke of deep thought . . . then suddenly realisation. 'Oh, yes! Twelve o'clock! Lunchtime!'

'We need to go to Queens'. How long will that take
please?'

'Twenny minutes.'

And we took his word for it. It didn't strike us for a
moment that in his mind, every journey might take
'Twenny minutes.' It would strike us soon enough.

* * *

An hour after checking into our rooms at the half-built
Best Western Hotel on Broadway, we were out on the
street again, looking for one of those legendary American
diners to stave off Tough Talk's constant hunger pangs
for a few hours. We found our reward at the end of the
street, and I was suddenly last in the queue.

'What's the house special?' I foolishly asked, as Adam
got excited about the buffalo burger.

'Pancakes and bacon' smiled the waitress, through
less-than-Hollywood dentistry.

This sounded good to me, especially after the heavy
workout (mouth and throat) I'd given myself in the car. I
immediately imagined thick succulent bacon rashers,
smothered perhaps in American cheese and enveloped
by Fajita-esque pancake wraps. After all, I wasn't stupid.
Over here, if they say chips, they mean crisps. If they say
pants, they mean trousers. So if they say pancakes, they
mean . . .

'Real pancakes?' I gasped as the heavy plate appeared
in front of me. 'I wasn't expecting real pancakes. I
thought they'd be . . . '

'What?' asked Steve. 'Roast beef and Yorkshire pud-
dings?'

The waitress returned, bearing further bad food news.

'And here's your maple syrup sir. Enjoy.'

I paused for a moment. Was I supposed to drink this?

Surely I wasn't supposed to put it on the bacon? A help-ful local confirmed my worst fears. So slowly, with one eye clapped shut in fear, I gently drizzled my fried pig in dessert sauce. Then, as my fork shook like a water divin-ing stick, I prepared myself for either a retch-inducing taste assault, or a pleasant surprise. And after taking that bite, I have one piece of advice, which may come in use-ful one day and might even surprise you: Don't do it, friends.

An hour later we were walking through the buzz and fuzz and lights and sights of Broadway, meeting some terrifically tall buildings and stupidly sizeable billboards. A few blocks along we found ourselves in Times Square – the busiest, brightest, most-commercial piece of land I've ever been overwhelmed by. On the in-flight movie, I'd watched Tom Cruise run through this place when it was completely empty – which of course turned out to be a hallucination. But strangely, that's what this place felt like – a drug-fuelled vision of the future; a picture more suited to Ridley Scott's *Bladerunner* than to real life. I remembered the first time I drew the curtains of that chalet in France – this was a similar experience in terms of my awe and wonder. But those mountains, fashioned by the Creator's hand, had been replaced here by an arti-ficial equivalent: magnificent but breakable structures, reaching up to heaven like miniature towers of Babel. And the reassuring natural darkness of Châtel could never be bright enough for the city that never sleeps, so instead a thousand shades of neon burn the tourist's eyes. But as this city knows better than most, tall build-ings can fall down. And light can be extinguished.

Chapter 6

East Coast

I was woken up by the impatience of the city that never sleeps – just like they'd warned us about in the song. Just before 6 a.m., after a night's sleep that had been broken, or rather, shattered by my perennial roommate's incessant wind-tunnel snoring, the assorted builders, birds and bums of New York City joined forces to make my bloodshot awakening permanent. Sinatra should have been more careful with what he wished for. In the other bed, short-straw Paul snored on, so, with a little time to myself, I sought my first daylight experience of the TV nation in thirty-five channels of hotel cable.

Rubbish. Rubbish. Spanish station. Rubbish. It wasn't difficult to see why Springsteen complained so vehemently about 'fifty-seven channels and nothing on'. Rubbish. Advert. Cartoon. Rubbish.

Then, finally, at the ninth attempt, I found something interesting. In a studio which claimed (via careful placement of a large still photograph) to overlook the Capitol Building, a starched little man sat almost inanimate as he talked sternly to camera. At the bottom of the screen, a caption written in suitably dull lettering managed to illuminate me on the focus of this very serious news programme. 'Does God have a special plan for America?' it asked, in half-hearted grey-on-black.

'What do you think?' he asked the entire East Coast, as passionately as one might address an entire old people's home. 'Does God have a special plan for us? Does he protect us and look after us more than he does any other country?' Like Russia, or China, or Terrorland, he inferred with wrinkled brow.

'Yes! Hallelujah, he's alive, he's alive, he is risen!' screamed a madman from Washington state.

'No! There's no such thing as God. We're destroying the planet by ourselves' argued a cheery soul from New Jersey.

Positives and negatives, God-squadders and heathens, flowed alternately through the switchboard with manufactured balance. At this early hour nobody seemed capable of saying anything of tremendous interest, save for the conspiracy theorist who tried to explain that it was in fact the FBI who blew up the Twin Towers, before being cut off. But it wasn't the content of the debate that I found so striking. Rather, I was shocked by its very presence on mainstream morning television. I mean, in the UK, this just wouldn't happen. You wouldn't catch Jeremy Bowen and Sophie Raworth, God bless 'em, discussing the possible Second Coming of Jesus on *BBC Breakfast News*. No, clearly there's a marked difference between them and us when it comes to matters of spirituality.

Paul stirred gruntily beside me, just in time to hear the starched newsman hasten through news of a shooting in Queens. With a bit of luck, they would clean up the blood before we got there.

* * *

'So how long did you say it would take to get to Queens from the hotel?'

'Twenny minutes.'

We'd left the hotel half an hour ago. We were nowhere near our destination. Dario was clearly bluffing.

'How long to get there from here please?'

Dario thought, long and hard.

'Twenny minutes.'

Ah.

Forty minutes later, after riding from the mountains of Manhattan to a land of two-storey familiarity, we were standing on a sunny sidewalk. It was midday, and we'd arranged to meet a man about a street outreach. As I understood it, Tough Talk were planning to take their cabaret to ghettoland, for an afternoon of weightlifting, Christian testimony, and bullet avoidance. Just ahead of us was a giant brick building, low on windows and shaped like a warehouse. This was Christ's Tabernacle, one of two churches who had invited Tough Talk out here to the Big Apple. For the next two days, we'd be seeing a lot of this place.

Of course, this wasn't Tough Talk's first visit to NYC: they'd been here twice before. The first time, they'd travelled over with a platoon of dancers, singers, musicians and performing monkeys, with whom they'd put on all-action shows all over the state. The second time, just two years ago, they'd brought a smaller team and worked closely with individual churches. One of those churches was Christ's Tabernacle of Queens, at the mighty foot of which we now stood.

They'd clearly made an impression first time around, for as the door swung open, a beaming young man of no more than twenty-five came leaping out towards them with arms outstretched.

'Pastor Adam!' shouted Arthur.

'Arthur!' shouted Pastor Adam, joining in the spirit of the movie moment and embracing his long-lost friend.

Fifteen reunions and introductions followed while we were ushered inside, away from the mean streets and into a junk-food paradise.

'We've got potato chips, cookies and soda – help yourselves!' proclaimed Pastor Adam, before continuing with the hugging and hand-shaking. Disappointingly, he'd been misinformed by the caterers. They actually had crisps, biscuits and Coca-Colas. But I wasn't prepared to correct one so full of love.

Pastor Adam, last name Durso, was a big, full-figured man. Shaven-headed and casually dressed, he looked about as much like a Reverend as he did a giraffe. His baggy T-shirt bore an indecipherable graffiti slogan, his – as they're called here – pants were loose and skateboard-friendly. Yet according to Arthur, who practically joined our two hands and shook them for us, he was 'an incredible man of God.' So was Charles Wesley, I thought, but at least he had the decency to dress up for it.

We all guzzled biscuits, cookies, crisps and chips together, regardless of our nationalities. More pastors (for there were many) filtered into the room and joined in the welcome. Then, when we'd all consumed enough calories, Pastor Adam called us together and asked for quiet. We formed an almost perfect circle, as if we were druids getting ready to sacrifice a small animal.

'First of all,' he began, with the vocal authority of one much older, 'I want to welcome you to New York, and to Queens, from the bottom of my heart. You can't know how excited I am to see you here, because I know that this weekend we're going to see a lot of things happen. I believe that God is with you people, and I believe that he's going to work through you in a big way while you're here.'

And then, grabbing the hands of the two people on either side of him, one of whom happened to be the utterly bemused Dario, and encouraging the rest of us to do likewise, he began to pray.

If you've ever watched television at Christmas, you've probably seen *Willy Wonka and the Chocolate Factory* a few hundred times. You may recall a famous scene, as Wonka leads his boat-bound factory guests into a bizarre psychedelic water tunnel, where they hurtle through experiences designed to engage and challenge and terrify every one of their senses. As they do so – wondering if they're heading at top speed towards impending doom – all Wonka can do is sing a scary little poem. 'There's no earthly way of knowing . . . ' he mutters, like Philip Larkin on Acid, 'which direction we are going . . . ' Understandably, Roy Kinnear and the rest of the guests become decidedly concerned. Then, as the boat (driven by two Oompa-Loompa's, you understand) picks up speed, Wonka's poem follows suit. 'THE ROWERS KEEP ON ROWING! AND THEY'RE CERTAINLY SHOWING NO SIGN OF SLOWING!' he screams, as they charge towards the climax. Then, suddenly there is calm and peace, and everyone opens their eyes and realises that everything is OK.

I relate this moment of movie magnificence because I can find no other way of adequately illustrating Adam Durso's prayer. He bowed his head, we closed our eyes. He started confidently; thanked God for our presence and our safe arrival, and got on with a bit of the old 'Lord you're so great, Lord you're so mighty' adoration. For the first thirty seconds or so, these words were uttered at an acceptable, if above-average volume. It didn't shock me: after all, I'd been around Ian and Arthur for quite a while now. But suddenly, just like the Oompa-Loompas, Pastor Adam decided to change gear. He shouted! He screamed!

He implored God to help Tough Talk on the streets;
he begged Him for protection in dangerous areas; he
beseeched Him that souls would be saved. The grip of
every hand-on-hand in our holy circle tightened and
tensed, just as Roy Kinnear had assumed the crash position. Then, swiftly, relievingly, calmly: 'Amen.' We were
all still OK. Our boat hadn't crashed.

After a few moments of communal shell shock, the
hands began to drop away. It was time for the mission to
begin.

'Dario!' called Arthur to the tall, startled Dominican
who'd been caught in the spiritual crossfire.

'Hello.'

'How long to get down there?'

'Five minutes.'

Now this was a shock. In the short space of time since
our arrival on American soil, Dario's sense of timekeep-
ing had already become established as a standing joke.
We'd all stood by listening to this conversation, waiting
for our cue to laugh as he tried to tell us that a ten-block
journey would take twenty minutes. But he didn't.

'Five minutes? Great,' enthused Arthur, excited that
even Dario would get us there with rapidity. 'Let's go.'

'Wait!' Dario urged. 'Can only take four people at a
time – only one car.'

Skip forwards if you've worked it out already.

'But there's sixteen of us!' Arthur despaired.

Dario counted in his head for a moment.

'I do four trips. Only five minutes to get there and
back.'

'Great,' said Arthur, 'then lets get going.'

'No problem. I get you all there in twenny minutes.'

Imagine a regular high street, complete with regular delicatessen, regular hamburger joint, regular coffee shop.

Now add shadows. Irregular shadows, on sidewalks, between buildings, behind trees. That's Queens: a safe and pleasant place haunted by invisible darkness. The newspapers and the stilted news anchors will tell you all about the shootings and the gangfights and the drugs and the hookers there. But you can't see them yourself – not with innocent, untrained eyes.

Tough Talk set up base in a very regular-looking patch of extended sidewalk at the edge of a busy road. There was a bus stop, a few benches and a big delicatessen nearby, and we were informed that if there was a community meeting point in Queens where young people would generally mill around, then this was it. A set of brand new weights had been delivered to the spot, courtesy of a sympathetic local gym, and so, by the time the nearby schools turned out for the weekend, the boys were all set up and raring to go.

The plan was to put on a similar demonstration to the one in Châtel, with powerlifting, story-telling and crowd interaction, but without the French translation. This time however, the focus of the affair was not self-contained. Instead, the men on the microphone would implore passers-by to join them in the evening, in the slightly less notorious surrounding of Christ's Tabernacle, for the worryingly-titled 'Youth Explosion' meeting. To emphasise the point, some of the trip's hangers-on – myself included – would be positioned amongst the crowd and on the sidewalk, giving out leaflets containing the same invitation. (There was a mix up in the translation though: the leaflets we were given bore the mugshots of Arthur, Ian and Steve alongside the logo 'The Power House Team'. I wasn't sure from where the confusion arose, but convinced myself that just as chips and biscuits must take on new monikers over here, so must imported evangelists.)

At around three o'clock, the familiar beats of Tough Talk's limited backing track began to echo around the 'hood. The battle-hardened local residents looked up in nervous surprise, and almost immediately the rapid response unit of the NYPD parked up opposite, sensing trouble. Yet the darkness remained in the shadows, and Arthur was able to grab the microphone and bid Queens a good afternoon.

'Come on!' he cried. 'Let's do it!'

And they did. It was like being in Châtel all over again, except without the unspoilt natural beauty.

I got my first chance to talk properly to Adam Durso as Marcus kicked off the bench-pressing competition. Behind us, Ian stood atop a low, sturdy wall, shouting encouragement to Marcus and attempting to engage with confused passers-by. A small crowd was beginning to gather, and understandably so. After all, It's not often that something like this happens in a place like Queens.

'This is quite a notorious area isn't it?' I asked Pastor Adam, whilst keeping a firm eye on my unattended bag.

'We have a lot of problems out here in Queens' he replied, glancing over at the harmless-looking deli-catessen. 'You see that place there?'

'Uh-huh.'

'That's a notorious drug spot. It's a pretty safe bet that if you walked in there right now and you knew where to look, you'd find a lot of things that shouldn't be there.'

'How do you know that?' I asked, fascinated by his insight and wondering why he hadn't passed on the information to someone in uniform.

'It's common knowledge. The police know about the place, and every so often they come and raid it, and shut it down. Then everything goes quiet for a while, and the deli reopens with a new name and a new set of faces.

Then after a few weeks, you get to hear that they're doing it all over again, and it's still a drug spot.' Adam puffed out his bottom lip in a strange grimace, and shook his head.

I looked over at the innocent fascia of the '24–7 Delicatessen'. People were walking in and out as if it was the most normal high street shop in the world. Perhaps to them it was. But now I knew its secret, and the shadow was no longer hidden from me. Suddenly there was a dark background hovering menacingly behind Tough Talk's street show. I cursed my sheltered Surrey upbringing, and went to stand a little closer to my muscle-bound friends.

By the time Steve Johnson had begun to tell his story, a sizeable crowd was beginning to clutter up the sidewalk. Looking on behind him, I'd positioned myself between the towering Gordon and the broad-shouldered Paul (I would forgive him all his snoring, I decided, if he protected me from any local drug-running knife maniacs who might happen to be out and about that afternoon). From my shelter, I took a good look at the crowd in order to get an idea of the local neighbourhood demographic. Almost instantly came the realisation that London is not quite the multicultural city that we Londoners like to pretend it is. Here in Queens, no two skin tones were the same – in a crowd of fifty people there must have been a double-figured number of nationalities. There were Hispanic people, black people, white people – but what do those limited terms tell us? These people, or their forefathers, came here from a thousand different places to help make up modern New York. It's not ghettoised, like TV cop shows still like to pretend, into large houses full of wealthy white Americans and squashed tower blocks full of angry Puerto Ricans. This place was a mosaic of people and their cultures. *West Side Story* now looks well out of date.

Steve's brief patter on life-changing experience procured a clutch of understanding nods from the growing throng. They appeared to be on Tough Talk's side now, and as he hung up the microphone in the, now brilliant, sunshine, it seemed like a good time to get them involved with some more lifting. Ian stepped forward and explained the rules of the latest challenge: whoever could keep an 80-kilo bar held upright for the longest from a standing start, would be the winner. (He didn't explain the prize – a Tough Talk New Testament – for painfully obvious reasons.) Adam McMillan, with sunglasses in place in an attempt to look like a pocket Schwarzenegger, stepped forward to demonstrate. He managed twenty seconds without too much bother, then coolly lowered the bar. Ian threw the competition open and found no end of takers.

Taking a step back from the situation for a moment, I was hit by the realisation that, actually, this was complete and utter madness. We'd come from London, a city with a big mouth but, ultimately, small trousers, with our padded jackets and our jarring big-beat dance music all packed in the suitcase. We'd crossed the Atlantic – some of us in luxury comfort – and installed ourselves in a Broadway hotel. Now Tough Talk were deep in one of the world's most notorious neighbourhoods, lifting weights and flaunting pretty wives and expensive video cameras. We were disturbing the peace, and what's more, playing music that this part of the world considered to be painfully out of date. We were in over our heads here. And as the sun beat down and made the polluted air quiver, I realised that nobody – but nobody – does this.

People don't come from overseas and preach to New York gang members in their own backyards. It reminded me a little of when the England football team won 5–1 in Germany. As Ray, my football watching-partner, had said to me in a near-delirious state that glorious night: 'that sort of thing just doesn't happen – nobody goes over there and does that to them.'

I retraced my backward step and saw a huge Hispanic man holding the loaded bar as if it were a polystyrene prop. It was Dario, our driver and now our friend, attempting to win what had turned into a popular lifting contest. Forty seconds moved him into third place – he barely even broke sweat. Fifty-five seconds saw him to within sight of the leader – he was still smiling. One minute came and went, and soon Dario was way out in front. Eventually, and presumably more through boredom than through pain, he allowed the bar to drop. He grinned and gave a deep laugh as Ian held his hand aloft, handing him his trophy. His excitement wasn't to be dented, even when he saw that he'd simply been presented with the lighter half of the Bible. He carried on beaming, because his prize was decorated with the face of Arthur, who after publicly deadlifting several-hundred pounds (for now Arthur lifted in both metric and imperial) had become his new hero.

* * *

Tough Talk had gone down pretty well in Queens. We'd handed out nearly all the mistitled fliers, and despite the fact that the *Spiderman* movie was due to hit theatres that night, Pastor Adam was of the opinion that many of the friends we'd made on the street would be coming back in the evening. Over the course of the afternoon literally hundreds upon hundreds of locals and passers-by had either stood and watched or (like French skiers) listened from a distance. Tough Talk had gone out into the community and made a big impression.

As, back at the Tabernacle, we sat and enjoyed a meal so big that it even defeated Paul, the Tough Talkers compared notes and stories on the afternoon's work. Steve, for instance, had convinced two passing Mormons to bench-press against each other. Paul, on the other hand, had got talking to an undercover cop, who'd told him that there were several drug-dealers, thieves and killers in the crowd. The occupant of every seat around the table had a different story to tell – having patched for one afternoon into the heartbeat of New York life.

Three vats of chicken, beef and deep-fried banana later, we were ushered into the main church auditorium. It was a vast room – an old converted cinema – with hundreds of plush red seats and a big balcony. At the front of the room, a well-proportioned stage, abundant in both width and depth, dominated the sanctuary. And all across the front wall, home-grown paintings and deliberate graffiti gave the place a creative and youthful edge. There must have been seven hundred seats in there. Conservatively we decided merely to colonise the front row with our big jackets and electrical equipment.

On stage, a choir of pretty young girls sang upbeat gospel numbers. On the balcony, sound technicians made sure of the acoustics. All around the building, little pockets of people were getting on with their jobs, making the preparations for the expected crowd's arrival. Taking the hint, Ian gathered the team together and began to talk through positions and responsibilities for the show. Arthur and Marcus began to gently flex their muscles. Quietly and dutifully as ever, Adam and Gordon began to set up the weights centre stage. Elsewhere, after sneaking away from the rest of the party, some of the dedicated prayer-people who'd travelled over with us were pacing around the place with heads bowed and arms outstretched, like actors rehearsing Shakespeare. This, said Jacqui, who appeared to be preparing for a run as Lady Macbeth at the National Theatre, was called prayerwalking. Before any major event, she and others like her would walk around a venue, praying for individual chairs and for the individuals who might sit in them later. She'd pray that they'd listen to the message, that it would make an impact on their hearts and minds, and that by the power of God they'd be compelled to respond. So, while Arthur took the plaudits as a powerlifter, his wife floated quietly around in the shadows as a prayerwalker. What's that phrase about 'behind every great man . . . '?

Prayer is, in fact, of great concern to the seasoned and serious evangelist. The assorted members of Tough Talk had, since I'd known them, been unashamed of the fact that at any moment, one of them might start rattling off requests and thankyous to the Almighty. On the way through France, for instance, Arthur would continually interrupt our vacuous conversation to thank God for the clouds, to ask for divine help to assist a motorist that we'd passed, whose car had broken-down, or simply to pray that we were on the right road. Prayer was obviously an explicit part of his life. It was clear that the locals at Christ's tabernacle also took the subject seriously. We were informed, on our arrival, that a prayer group had been meeting regularly in the run-up to our visit to the States, with the sole purpose of asking God for a safe and successful mission. And while the team was on stage that night, a similar group would be meeting downstairs, praying prayers of petition throughout.

But first, and in the same Spirit, it was time for everyone involved in the evening event to gather together.

Pastor Adam took the stage and addressed the assorted
powerlifters, band members, stewards and welcomers.
Again, he began to pray. Again, he recreated that classic
Willy Wonka moment. But as he finished, a hundred
voices – young and old; black, white and Hispanic – leapt
into action. Now I'd been shocked by assertive praying
twice before – once at Chez White, and once in the ring-
o'-roses situation earlier that day. I had been pretty sure
that listening to people talk to God would never again
surprise me. That was until now. They clapped, they
shouted, they sang, they shook. They completely blew
my mind.

Five minutes before the event was due to start, I couldn't
resist poking my head around the proverbial 'safety cur-
tain'. Slipping through a gap in the security, I found
myself on the same patch of sidewalk that had earlier
greeted us on arrival. But whilst back then this had
belonged to an empty street, now it was overrun with
excited chatter. Around the block, a queue snaked as if
Spiderman was to premiere here, and not in Manhattan
after all. Attracted by those glossy fliers, they'd come in
their droves – in all shapes, sizes, smells and colours.
And when, in Queens, you talk about colours, you're not
just referring to skin. We'd known in advance that many
of tonight's audience would be gang members, and
therefore would arrive in their appropriate branding.
Sure enough there were yellow headbands, red headbands, blue, green and so on, bobbing and swaggering in
the unruly line. But the young faces underneath weren't
quite what a world raised on Spike Lee movies might
expect them to be. Some of them belonged to mere
children – ten and twelve year olds – sucked into the
darkened depths of gang culture because acceptance was
forthcoming from no other place. It was a sad sight, and

though I may be no prayerwalker, I had a simple request for the man upstairs. I didn't care, in the first instance, if these people were 'brainwashed' into following Jesus that night. But looking at them there, in all their decaying innocence, I prayed that through hearing the Tough Talk stories they might realise that they had a choice.

The ground floor of the auditorium filled quickly and noisily, mainly with the wide-eyed, banded heads from outside, but also with a fair sprinkling of latecomers, all of more advanced years. In the seat directly behind mine, an enormous man covered in questionably-originated jewellery planted himself down at possibly the last available moment before the house lights went down. He looked like your stereotypical gunrunning drug boss. Possibly he was.

The evening kicked off with an assault on the senses, and mainly the ears. The Lordz Knights – a group of young rappers from within the church – belted out two self-penned tracks with all the poise and attitude that one might expect from the expletive-obsessed 'real thing'. We stood, we clapped, we generally didn't know what to do with ourselves. (This just isn't the sort of thing that we're used to in England. Back home, a 'Youth Explosion' meeting would probably involve a few cupcakes and some Tesco cola.) As we got into the catch of the sampled backing track, I began to swing in a slightly less contrived manner (to the locals however, I still probably looked like I was doing the funky chicken), and started to listen to the lyrics. Impressed by the production levels, I expected a string of F-words to leap forth from the mouths of these angry young men. Instead, in songs like 'My brothers you need the Lord', they merely hit us with a barrage of J-words. Eminem would never get anywhere near the Radio 1 playlist if he went around using language like that.

In many ways these boys in baggy clothes and jangling medallions were the best possible warm-up act. They were local lads, and so they automatically got the audience on side. They were making music, so they got everyone moving. And they were only on for ten minutes, which left the crowd pleading desperately for further entertainment. So when Pastor Adam got a hold of the microphone, and introduced the 'Power House Team', the former cinema erupted, just as it might have done after the first showing of *Star Wars*, back in its former life. Ian sent Sean O'Boyle, a lover of youth culture and street slang, on to introduce the team under their proper name. So, in his best attempts to sound down-with-the-youth, Sean explained who we had 'in the house', told us that they'd be 'keeping it real', and generally said things like 'aiiiii'. Since he used to run illegal raves before his conversion to Christianity, this sounded surprisingly half-decent, and only helped to further excite the 400-plus spectators. Then, with the whole team on stage, stretching in a near-perfect line of standard-issue jackets across the width of the auditorium, he handed the wand to Arthur, who added a few words of welcome before beginning to tell his story.

'Hello Queens!' he milked, as the less-than-popular Tough Talk dance anthem continued to ring out behind him. The assembled masses were a forgiving bunch, and despite a commonly-felt distaste for the music, they screamed with delight anyway.

'We're a bunch of ordinary men, but we serve an extraordinary God. His name is Jesus Christ. Come on!' The music continued to blare. Arthur shouted himself hoarse over the top of it before, up on the balcony, the soundmen finally saw the penny drop. At last the music faded.

'My name is Arthur White – I work with a team of people called Tough Talk. We're a registered non-profit-making organisation from the UK, and we've come here tonight to tell you some stories about how our lives were changed. As you can see, we're a bunch of ordinary men but, as I said, we've all encountered an extraordinary God.' His eyes darted across to Marcus, now stripped of the regulation 'puffa' jacket, standing with one hand on the loaded bar. 'Are we ready to go? We're gonna lift some weights tonight – we're gonna see some big weights lifted. Here's Marcus coming out to squat first of all. We're gonna see him lift over six hundred pounds. Let's give Marcus some support!'

So Arthur had barely started telling his story before he'd allowed himself to be interrupted. As I've mentioned before, they don't teach you this approach down at Bible college. Marcus squatted with consummate ease. Arthur continued from where he'd left off:

'You know, as Sean introduced me, he told you that I'd been six-time British powerlifting champion. I'm the current British Champion – won the last one just last weekend. I've been four-time European and twice World Champion. I've been in the Guinness Book of Records between 1982 and 1999. I've broken somewhere in the region of fifty or sixty British, European and World records, a number of which I still hold. But let me tell you something – I'd sacrifice everything I've ever won, to know Jesus Christ. Ten years ago He stretched His hand out and He dragged me out of the pit. He stood me on the rock, which is His word, and He set me free.

'Are you ready to go Marcus?'

Marcus lifted again, making it look a hundred times more difficult than was truthfully the case. Then the focus switched back.

'Come on! Give him a clap, he's doing good! Now let me say this: we haven't travelled here to patronise, to talk down, to preach or teach at you. We just want to have some fun with the weights. When we came last time, there were some strong guys, and some strong girls, so we want some volunteers in a minute. [Cue uproar from crowd.] Sit down – sit down! Not yet! Now listen up. Powerlifting was my God – this is what I worshipped. My whole life revolved around powerlifting – when I arrived on my honeymoon after getting married, the first thing I did was find the nearest gym. But my obsession had a high price, and I ended up getting involved in the taking of anabolic steroids and cocaine. For between eight and ten years, I was a drug addict – hooked. As a direct result of that addiction, I lost everything that ever meant anything to me. In six years, I blew $250,000 on my cocaine addiction – now that's a lot of money. I had an adulterous affair with a young woman – I left my wife and lost my children. I lost my homes, my business, my jobs, my cars, my money – and somehow I still thought I was in control of my life, and yet the drugs were controlling me.

'We've got on the bar over three hundred pounds. This is getting serious.'

It seemed a bizarre moment to shy away from the focus. Arthur was pouring his heart out here – he'd obtained the quiet attention of every person in the room, including Mr T behind me. Suddenly the music was pumping again, and we were looking at Marcus pretending to have difficulty with what he'd consider a warm-up weight. One thing was for sure though. When Arthur started talking again, he'd have our undivided attention.

'Come on! I'm the old one on the team – they drag me around with them to make themselves look good. In fact, I won my first British title twenty-one years ago – I bet some of you weren't even born then. I got involved in the taking of steroids and cocaine, and that is what ruled and was ruining my life. Nine of my good friends – all bodybuilders and powerlifters – died through steroid and cocaine addictions. I thought I was in control of my life, and yet my life was out of control. Everybody else was doing it, so that's what I did. You choose your friends wrong, you choose to run with the wrong crowd, and believe me you'll be dragged down.

'My heart ballooned to the size of a small football due to the drugs – it was going to explode. I attempted suicide on a number of occasions. There were men in the East End of London who were gonna take my life. My life ten years ago was over: there was only one way for me to go, and that was down, and that was death. My life was finished – I'd lost my homes, my wife, my business, my jobs, my cars, my money, my family. Materialistically, everything that meant anything to me, I lost. And yet I still thought I was in control of my life. There's a consequence for your actions. If you choose wisely in life you'll have a glorious one. If you choose wrongly, then you'll end up in the same place that I could have ended up.

'Are you ready Marcus? We've now got 420 pounds on the bar.'

Mouths were open here. The crowd desperately wanted to hear how Jesus Christ, or anyone, could have possibly got Arthur out of such a mess. But their attention was divided now, for as Arthur was speaking more and more weight was being added to Marcus's bar. It was an intriguing sub-plot, for it was the weights that many people had come to see – a glance around at the assembled musclemen in the audience told us that much. Now this was a lot of weight, whether you talk in pounds or kilos, and so interest levels were roof high behind almost every single pair of eyes. The spiritually hungry were hanging on Arthur's every word. The muscle-heads were desperate to see Marcus squat some more. Suddenly, I understood the logic behind Tough Talk's rule-breaking approach.

'Ten years ago,' continued Arthur, 'my life was almost at an end. I was running an illegal debt-collecting business in the East End of London. I used to carry a twelve-inch divers knife strapped to my forearm, and I would draw and use that knife as I needed. I remember stabbing a guy twice outside a club. I stabbed him twice in the back, I pinned him to the floor, and I started to cut his ear off. I didn't want to kill him, but I needed to teach him a lesson – that's the sort of thing that I was doing then. But a voice called out to me to stop. And I got up – there was a crowd as big as what's here tonight – the crowd parted, I got in my car and drove off. Looking back I now know that God was speaking to me.

'My heart ballooned, as I said, to the size of a small football. A doctor told me that I was going to die. My addiction was killing me – just like it had killed my nine friends. As I keep telling you, my life was over ten years ago. My wife, who's here in the audience tonight, said I needed help, and pointed me in the direction of a counsellor, who happened to be a Christian. Now ten years ago I didn't think too much of Christians. I thought they were wimps. Why did they wear sandals, these Christian men? And they wore socks with their sandals – although I've still never fathomed that one.

'Marcus Williams has got over five hundred pounds on the bar. . . .'

Marcus was really playing to the crowd now. He allowed the music to crescendo, he waited for the support to flourish. Bending the bar on purpose with his shoulders, he grimaced his way through another three squats.

'Now I went to see this Christian guy because I didn't think he'd be too much trouble to me. I was a guy with a bit of street-cred – I could look after myself and I knew how to protect myself. So I still took the knife with me. I had it strapped to my leg just in case he hit me with a Bible. You see I wasn't into this Bible-bashing, these Christians. But he said to me one thing as I left him. He said, 'You need to choose.' And we all have choices to make. We had to choose to travel three and a half thousand miles – not to preach to you – but to share with you something special in our lives. We have to choose, and as I said to you, if you choose wrongly, you're going to have a disastrous life. Choose wisely, and you could have a glorious one. Ten years ago, I stood in a freezing cold car park, in the East End of London. On my own – not in a church, not with a minister – and I asked God to come into my life. There was no booming voice, no opening of the heavens, no choirs of angels. But something happened. Because for the first time in years, the paranoia went from my life. For the first time in years, fear went from my life. I became a born-again Christian.

'Whether you choose to believe or not is up to you. But no one can argue with the truth of my life. Since I invited Jesus Christ into my life He healed me – He healed my swollen heart. He healed my marriage. He gave me back a life. And I'm competing again – I'm lifting weights and I'm British Champion. And I'm drug free.

'Marcus, come on!'

Marcus readied himself for the final, huge weight. Admittedly, this was not an easy lift, and Marcus was possibly only one of three men in the room capable of successfully squatting it. The crowd, now on their feet as one and buoyed by the happy resolution to Arthur's story, positively belted out encouragement by the bucketful. On either side of him, just in case, Adam and Gordon stood anxiously with catching-arms outstretched. Marcus ducked under the bar and took the strain. He descended, with sweat pouring from his forehead – this was no longer for show. Letting out the shout of a true actor though, he rose magnificently from the dip. He returned the bar to its stand, then punched the air as the crowd fell into demented applause. It ceased very quickly however, as Arthur took the microphone for his conclusion:

'I had a choice to make ten years ago. There aren't many Christian sayings that I like. But you know, at the age of forty-one, my life was over, and I was 'born again'. You may not understand that, some of you young people – you've got a long way to go to catch me up. But I'm telling you: to be 'born again' is the greatest feeling I've ever had. I've won many trophies in my time but I'd give them all up. I've never known such a feeling as being filled with the Holy Spirit.

'If anybody tells you that being a Christian is gonna make your life rosy then they're not telling you the truth. But I would not go back to the life that I once had. I believe it takes a stronger man or woman, boy or girl to follow Jesus Christ than it does to run from Him. And I believe that as a Christian, I'm a bigger man today than I ever was before. Thanks for listening.'

Moments later, a bench-pressing competition between kids with rival headbands worked the crowd to bursting-point. Then Steve restored decorum by beginning to tell his tale, and Arthur began to demonstrate his lifting credentials, as Marcus had before him. Again, the picture on stage alternated like the stripes on a crossing. And when Steve had finished, drawing gasps and grins from the young faces as he went, Ian took the floor and delivered a hard-hitting Christian message. The bottom line – or the hard sell, in timeshare terms – was an open invitation for people to buy into Christianity.

If Ian ever grows too old for static guarding, there may be a career for him at one of the television shopping channels. With his permanent tan, immaculate hair and chiselled features, he may look menacing, but add his near-constant smile to that mix, and suddenly you have a face capable of selling expensive lifestyle accessories with real sincerity. Here, with microphone in hand, Ian could easily have been trying to present a revolutionary type of stain remover to the audience. Although, thinking about it, he might argue that this was exactly what he was doing.

The response to Ian's simple plea was quite astonishing. There was no hint of brainwashing, as had been my fear: all had gone quiet; any hysteria was draining away. In fact, the approach was straight out of Bertolt Brecht's didactic theatre: the audience had been presented with all the facts – now they were being asked to make a decision on them. One by one, as Ian made his altar call, hands of all shapes, sizes and colours began to reach, rather aptly, toward heaven. Twenty hands, then thirty . . . forty . . . fifty – stuck out into the breezeless air. So, I thought, as after prompting from Ian the fifty owners of those fifty hands made their way to join Tough Talk at the front, this was it. This was what they called the giving of lives. After London, France and the Manchester mistake, I was finally ready to taste the pudding for proof. An eighth of the audience had assembled at the foot of the stage, where the men in grey puffa jackets had come down to meet them. This was the real deal – fifty people had heard the stories of Ian, Arthur and Steve, and made an identification with them. Somehow, these three men from London had made the supernatural seem natural and the invisible seem visible to them. And as fifty people laughed, wept and told their stories, I repented for ever having doubted Tough Talk.

Another twenny minute Dario drive took us home for
the night, and as I wavered between sleep and wake,
someone told an amazing story. Apparently, earlier that
evening, somewhere in deepest darkest Queens (and
possibly somewhere near the 24–7 Delicatessen), a young
gang member had been commissioned to perform a
drive-by shooting in a local neighbourhood. In order to
prove his commitment to the gang, he'd been asked
to assassinate another young man with a different head-
band and a different set of problems. Faced with no alter-
native – you simply don't let your gang down in this city
– he'd accepted his calling. But instead of heading
straight for the crime scene, this little hoodlum had set
off ahead of schedule so that he could check out the muscles on the much-advertised Power House Team, whose
leaflet he'd earlier been handed. His plan was to catch
the first part of the youth meeting from eight, leaving
well before his planned nine o'clock 'hit' time, when he
would get his murderous show on the road. But nine
o'clock came and went, and the gunman stayed in his
seat. The offer of salvation came forth, and so did he. The
shooting never took place, and the boy became a gang-
deserting Christian.

Tough Talk had saved two lives at once, but for that
one story there were forty-nine others. The people who
had made commitments to Christianity that night were
not from all walks of life – otherwise they wouldn't have
been there in the first place. These were hardened young
people from a hard-knock area, and that night, as we
made our way back to comfortable Manhattan, they
would be taking their new-found faith back to the ghet-
to's broken homes and streets from whence they came.
Life would still be difficult for them, just as Arthur had
warned. But tonight, as they deadlocked their doors to
danger and bolted their windows from the cold, there

would be a new hope in their hearts. I said a quiet prayer for all of them, and melted into sleep as we passed a sky-scraper skyline with two missing teeth.

Chapter 7

A Ravin' Lunatic

The next morning, I entered the waking world with a soundtrack of superficial sounds ringing in my ears. New York's premier breakfast DJ team – Elvis and Scary, apparently – were playing all the manufactured American pop that I'd hoped to leave behind in England. Paul woke too, somehow roused from his noise-polluting slumber by the same combination of soulless love songs and ten-in-a-row advertisements. We looked at each other from across the room, waved, and simultaneously reached for the off-button on our clock radio. I got there first, but the speed of my movement lacked co-ordination or control. So instead of stopping the noise completely, I only succeeded in changing the station. Now we had talk radio instead. The sound of an unlikely voice stopped me from taking another swing at the mass of buttons on the device.

'I think the events of 9/11 have damaged this city irrevocably,' said the Englishman, with words that instantly cemented themselves in my brain. 'The people who were in New York on that day will probably never, ever recover. It will take the emergence of an entirely new generation to wipe the slate clean.'

At once, a cluster of American voices rose to offer their agreement. 'So true!' gushed one. 'Very insightful!' spouted another. Paul's heavy fist slammed the snooze button before any more truth or insight could flow forth into our airwaves. It didn't matter. In ten seconds I'd gleaned two important pieces of information. First, this city was still licking its wounds in a big way, with all its inhabitants still on the road to recovery; and second, a British accent in New York will get you a long way.

London is famed for having a completely inadequate set of roads running through it. There are highways and byways, ring roads and circulars all the way around and to the side of it, but when it comes to navigating your way right through the centre, you'd have more luck with the old camel and needle trick. There are streets in London in the same sense that there were streets there two hundred years earlier, and unless you're on foot or shuttling around like a mole on the Underground, then you might as well forget it.

New York, by comparison, is full of ridiculously large thoroughfares. Giant roads, as wide as the Cheshire cat's grin, are standard in the city. Broadway itself is much akin to the M1, but with shops and theatres and mega-billboards all along the side. As we pulled off towards Queens again, this time for a men's breakfast, we got to take a ride on a few of these gigantic, pot-holed monstrosities. And as we did so, traversing the giant spider's web of avenues and streets and rattling along surfaces that were far too vast to be properly looked after, the reason for all this width became clear. American cars only come in one size, much like their trousers, and in both cases it's extra large.

Dario was quieter that morning. Perhaps it was the monotony of the roads; perhaps it was the monotony of the passengers. Whatever it was, it had taken UB40 and George Michael off the Lincoln's playlist. All the anglophile stuff had been replaced by some hardcore Hispanic hits. And despite producing some fine cigars and some excellent taxi drivers, when it comes to music, the Dominicans are no world leaders. We nodded our heads at the Bontempi organ beats, and attempted to join in with the Eurovision-esque patterns of 'ooh', 'aah' and 'la la la'. After a few songs Dario grew pleased with us, and with our acceptance of his culture. He too joined in with the nursery noisemaking. Then, as the final tune of a short but sweet collection drew to a close, I handed him a CD of my favourite music. And I learned an important lesson from the spitting and grimaces that followed: never give a big Dominican cab driver Crowded House.

We were back outside Christ's Tabernacle by eight, and stepped back onto its sidewalk moat less than nine hours after leaving it. A welcome party of eager young men beckoned us inside, clearly enthused by the stories they'd heard of the night before.

After setting up in the sanctuary again – Ian with his plan of action; Gordon and Adam with their silent work; Jacqui & Co. rehearsing Shakespeare – it was time for the much-anticipated breakfast. The veterans of Tough Talk had enjoyed these meetings before, and had spent much of the early morning raving and salivating about the food. It sounded like there was plenty to look forward to. Although in England churches run breakfasts for men, the organisers generally operate using a different recipe to their cousins across the sea. A men's breakfast in the garden of Europe is rarely free, and usually consists of one or two croissants and a plastic cup of tepid tea. In the 'land of the free' they do things another way.

'Bacon sir?' asked the keeper of the first food-vat.

I nodded as four crisp pink rashers moved from her trough to mine.

'Egg?' enquired the next smile.

I returned the expression, and got two servings for my trouble. I shared similar scripts with the potato and sausage people, and then, holding my sagging paper plate in both hands, staggered to the nearest seat. Opposite it was Steve Johnson, the thug-shaped gentleman with whom I'd spent so little time. He was staring glumly at the grease-factory on his plate, but he appeared to be concerned by more than just the heart attack which consuming it could possibly give him.

'You alright Steve?' I asked, through a mouthful of the most spectacular scrambled egg ever to originate from a four by two-foot container.

He chewed on a particularly brittle strip of meat, and it instantly shattered on his lips. A few crumbs of rind spiralled floorwards, but he managed to catch them on his plate. They wouldn't go to waste.

'I'm alright,' gurgled Steve. 'I just miss my family. My wife an' kids.'

'Oh, right. Me too.' We both looked into our plates and wondered: me about whether I'd manage to finish it all; him about whether they'd be offering seconds.

'My missus,' he said 'you should see her. She's beautiful. I know you wouldn't believe it, looking at a face like mine, but it's true.'

If I was painfully honest, looking at a face like his, I did find it hard to believe. Steve is a giant man, possibly bigger and heavier than anyone else on the team. He doesn't lift, but the menace in his battered face demands enough respect to make crowds listen when he talks. He's been a bouncer, a drunk and a soldier, and his face tells that weary story like an old tree stump with a hundred age-rings. So if I was honest, yes, it was hard to believe that this beast had somehow landed a beauty. As it was, my non-committal grunt seemed to satisfy him.

'I fank God for her every day. I spent too many years messin' her about, but fank God she stuck wiv me.'

True love was never plainer, even through Steve's minefield of glottal stop and lazy tongue. Although viewed through suffering, his emotions had an unexpected beauty. He'd been separated from his family for less than forty-eight hours, yet already his heart was heavy enough to burst. And considering, as I later discovered, where he'd come from, that really was remarkable.

'It is an absolute privilege to be here in New York City', bellowed Steve as he paced the stage an hour later. 'Alongside London, I would say it is one of the greatest cities in the world. It's my fird visit here, an' I'm humbled by the attention an' the welcome we get from you people. Because as Arfer's already said, we're just common guys, oo come from very very dodgy backgrounds, oo've come to know the love of Jesus Christ. An' it's a privilege too for me to be able to tell you, very briefly, my story. My name's Steve, an' I come from East London.'

This was an older but, at times, no less riotous crowd. They were men, and many of them were big, strong, hard men. Over breakfast, even Arthur had commented that he 'wouldn't like to meet one of these big lumps on a cold dark night.' So they were big men. They were the men of Queens, invited by friends and neighbours to escape the constant crises of ghettos and hard-knock living for one morning of Christian love. And they'd certainly been loved – in the truest biblical sense of the word – plenty already. And they'd had seconds.

This assembled assortment of stories and raw life experience watched Steve closely as he moved around the now graffiti-free stage, just as they had Arthur for the previous fifteen minutes. Hawk-eyed, they scrutinised him as he began to tell his tale – a tale which had more than a passing degree of relevance to their own.

'I come from a background where I'm the oldest of five children,' boomed Steve in an accent which many presumed to be Australian. 'I've got somefin' like twenty uncles. An' where I was from the culture was boozin'.'

'You know what boozin' is?' he asked.

'Gettin' drunk as often as possible' he answered. 'Now I'm not here to criticise anybody, or to have a comment on social drinkin'. But because my farver an' granfarver were drunks, by the time I was fifteen or sixteen – long before the legal age of drinkin' in a pub in England, but being a big guy I could always get into a pub an' get served – I became an 'eavy drinker. That was at the age of fifteen or sixteen when I should've been at school – it is not to be recommended. That led me onto a parf. Alcohol – the abuse of alcohol – ruined nearly every decision in my life. I walked out of school, an' then went from job to job to job, because I was unqualified. I listened to nobody. I listened to nuffin' apart from my own ego. An' eventually, I was gettin' drunk seven nights a week.'

Whilst the now-engrossed crowd pondered how your 'farver' and 'grandfarver' can lead you down a 'parf', Arthur reappeared at the front of stage. This time he had shed his muscle-hiding jacket and, encouraged by Ian on the microphone, he attempted an average deadlift. All eyes swapped from Steve, to Arthur, to Steve – like a crowd watching a tennis rally.

'Oo knows what a pub bouncer is?' asked Steve. 'You 'ave 'em in New York?'

A group of men, far too excited for this time of the morning, shouted 'yeah man!' in eerie unison. Everyone else just nodded their heads.

'Well when, as a young man, I was offered a job as a pub bouncer I fought it was the best day of my life. Because while I was prepared to hang around in bars gettin' drunk at my own expense, now somebody was prepared to pay me to do it. An' that was in the days when there was nuffin' legal abaat bein' pub security – goin' back a few years in London, if you were big enugh you got the job.

'Now alcohol, an' the abuse of alcohol, 'ad fuelled my aggression. An' we as a team of bouncers caused more fights than we ever stopped. We were nuffin' but trouble an' before I knew it, I started gavering a string of criminal convictions. An' I'll tell you somefin' briefly now: there's nuffin' abaat my past that I'm proud of. I don't tell these stories to boost my own ego. I'm still ashamed of the life that I was involved in, but we 'ave to tell you 'ow we were and tell you 'ow we are now, to explain the miracle that 'appened in between.'

That was important: a telling-off to anyone who'd come along purely to hear stories of blood and guts. I wrote it down in my pocket-book.

'I was a pub bouncer for many years. I've got fifty-nine stitches in my face, an' forty in the rest of my body. I've broken many bones in my 'ands through fightin'. I've served two prison sentences. I've been arrested forty, fifty, sixty times for crimes of drunkenness an' violence. I've lost caant – it was a way of life – an' I was actually nuffin' special where I was from, 'cause most of me family were that way. Booze fuelled an anger wivin me. I even travelled England, fightin' at football matches – football 'ooliganism is a scourge on our country, an' a few years ago I was a big part of that. That was my life, I was on a road to 'ell – boozin', gettin' arrested regularly an' neglectin' everybody decent araand me.'

Arthur strode out unassumingly for another lift. Many of the spectators were very well-built men, but even they were impressed to see that many metal plates on each end of the bar. Aware of his responsibility not to distract too much attention from the crux of Steve's story, he worked quickly and quietly. Then, after successfully completing the exercise, he chipped the ball back over the net and into his friend's end of the court.

'This kind of life,' continued Steve, 'in the pubs an' clubs of London, led me into working for criminal gangs. I turned up for work one day in East London an' instead of bein' presented wiv the usual weapons that we used to carry – a cosh, ammonia, knuckle-dusters – at the age of twenty-eight I was presented wiv a loaded gun an' a bullet-proof vest. An' that night a man was shot an' injured in East London by a friend of mine. That was the way my life 'ad gone – from this young guy 'oo liked to drink; to a pub bouncer because he could do nuffin' else; to lovin' to fight; to suddenly carrying guns an' driving araand wiv well-known criminals in London. This is a very brief description of 'ow my life was – believe me it was a lot, lot worse. All the time I was neglectin' my wife an' children, an' drinkin' over an 'undred pints of lager a week – an' that's a lot of drink.'

The audience showed agreement through a chorus of whistles and sighs. Steve's story was hard going, just like Arthur's. Fortunately, he'd reached the peak of the mountain, and it was time to run down the other side.

'But now I'm gonna tell you some good news. One day at my place of work, a stranger appeared – a professional boxer. We told each other abaat our backgrounds an' 'ee could see that I was what we would call a "ravin' lunatic". An' this man, 'oo was from a similar background to me, a short, stocky man wiv a shaved 'ead, smovered in tattoos, a professional boxer, 'ad the courage to say to me: "Steve I

was a bit like you once. But Jesus Christ changed my life."
That was the beginnin' of the rest of my life. I obviously
fought he was crazy. But over a period of abaat two or free
years, this man became a very good friend of mine. One
Christmas, havin' given myself a near-cripplin' back
injury where I couldn't walk, this man called me to his
office. I went under duress – because I was embarrassed
by 'is Christianity – but I went so that 'ee could pray for
me, for my injury. This man, this boxer, put 'is hands on
my shoulders an' prayed for me in the name of Jesus
Christ. I was 'ealed of a cripplin' back injury. Time passed
by. I'm not gonna tell you that that changed me – I was
confused, I was completely off the rails.

'Christmas 1996: when fings were takin' a turn for the
worse, I'd got a charge made against me which in
England is called 'grievous bodily 'arm with intent'. It's
only abaat two steps daan from murder. My own lawyer
told me that I would get seven years in prison. I didn't go
to prison that day, but at a time when my life was in a
complete mess, I prayed for the first time. I prayed, wiv
no Christian background, no knowledge of God. But I
prayed, Christmas 1996, for God to come into my life . . .
for Jesus Christ to heal me of a twenty-free year drink
addiction. I can say to you in all honesty – I 'aven't come
'ere free an' a 'arf fousand miles to lie to you – Jesus
Christ took away that twenty-free year alcohol addiction.
The 5th January 1997, I asked Jesus Christ to come into my
life – to guard me an' guide me an' lead me on. The last
five an' a 'arf years 'ave been the most productive years
of my life. Gettin' to know Jesus 'as restored every hope
an' every dream that I ruined when I was a teenager. An'
all I can say to you, as Arfer 'as said already, is this: it
takes more of a man to follow Jesus Christ than it does to
run from 'im. You can still be a real man an' follow Jesus.
The best day of my life was the day I was born again.'

Again, Ian closed the meeting by telling a few stories of
his own and making an appeal. There were close to four
hundred men in that room, and just as before around
forty or fifty of them made a physical response. Drug
addicts, killers, or underpaid labourers, each had been
touched by the message of hope. Pride fell by the way-
side, even in an area where pride is everything, and the
bulky figures of broken men filtered out of their rows,
into the aisles and down to the front of the sanctuary.
Again, the jacketed powerlifters stepped down to greet
them. And there were hugs, there were tears, and there
were prayers for salvation.

You possibly haven't experienced the true power of
the Christian message until you've seen six and a half
foot of hardened gangster sobbing uncontrollably in
another man's arms. That's what I saw.

As we waited for Dario and his friend to turn up with
their carriages, we guzzled chips and soda in the midday
sun. We must have looked quite a sight, there on that
sidewalk in Queens – a mass of bags and boxes, of tight
fitting T-shirts and reddening necks. Fifteen of the most
unlikely missionaries and me, out in the field, catching
the rays and the unwelcome stares. As I looked at my
watch and did the maths, I realised that I'd just missed
the FA Cup Final for the first time in my life.

Out of nowhere, a tall, well-built man with a face like
death infiltrated our group, making a dejected beeline for
Arthur. They spoke out of my earshot, but as they did so,
I noticed a tear running down the man's cheek. More followed, and as he struggled to speak he was quickly
surrounded by the compassionate faces of three more of
the team. Paul, who was standing close to me, expressed
an opinion that he'd seen this face at the meeting earlier.
Then we both strained our ears in an attempt to discover

more. I distinctly heard the words 'September 11th' emanate from his general direction. Paul reported that he'd lip-read 'Ground Zero'. The circle of men closed up, muffling any further sounds. They were praying for him, in their loud and unabashed way, right there on the street.

Ten minutes later, the man bade us all farewell. His eyes had puffed up; his cheeks were swollen. But there was a wide smile on his face now, a supernaturally different expression to the one he'd worn minutes earlier. Arthur, who's own visage displayed similar emotion, bounced over to us with an explanation. The man had spent the last eight months of his life labouring at the former site of the World Trade Center. He'd spent nearly a year finding disassembled body parts of fragmented people. And whilst he'd been a man of faith before that fateful event, the day-to-day experiences of working at Ground Zero had left him seriously disturbed. Now, when he woke up in the morning, he'd almost completely lost track of what he thought, let alone what he believed. As the wise old Englishman on the radio had hypothesised, he was wounded: one of the millions of living, breathing, walking wounded that now reside in this city. But this morning, three hours at Christ's Tabernacle had set him back on his feet. He hadn't been wowed by Marcus's muscles, or found identification with Arthur's cocaine story. What he'd seen was a group of Christians who had presented their faith in a real and tangible way. They'd kept it simple, but they'd kept it real. And suddenly, things started to make a bit more sense to him again. He was able to get perspective. So, passing back through the neighbourhood later on, and seeing Tough Talk perched oddly on the sidewalk, he'd asked them to pray for him. And by the end of those prayers this burnt-out husk of a man had been filled with an uncontrollable joy. Something, or someone, had given him the energy he needed to return to his work at Ground Zero.

A little way off now, I could still see his re-strung figure half-skipping at the end of the street. He was on his way out of Queens, in the general direction of Manhattan. In the general direction of Ground Zero. It was our afternoon off, and time to head in that direction ourselves.

* * *

Silence. An absolute, unnatural silence. People everywhere but none daring to speak. Service trucks speeding past on a craterous temporary road, too embarrassed to make a sound. Workmen and volunteers, digging and burrowing and hoping not to find what they're looking for. Silent, unreal, terrifying. Eight months after its unwanted birth, a place full of unheard screams and dried up tears. More heart-stopping than the pictures, more choking than any writer's description, this was the stuff of nightmares: Ground Zero.

Saturday afternoon had fallen into place as our sightseeing time. Half of our group had wisely taken the opportunity to get some shopping done, if only to check out that urban myth about the price of Levi's. Half of what was left had hotfooted it to Canal Street, famous home of the fake watch, fake shirt and fake handbag. In the world of full-price reality, only Arthur, Jacqui and myself remained. And there was only one place in this city that I wanted to go.

It's almost impossible to overestimate the effect that September 11th had on New York. The famed brashness of the native New Yorker has dimmed severely – replaced in part by nervousness and angst. The cabs are rarely reckless; the street performers subdued. Even Times Square, with its neon overdose and unadulterated largeness, is scared to operate at full volume. It's as if the whole city has been fitted with a pacemaker, and been told to avoid strenuous exercise for the foreseeable future.

The gift shops of Manhattan are all dominated by variations on the same theme: hats, shirts, scarves, models, pens, cigarette lighters and shot glasses. The World Trade Center, a now non-existent building that once dominated a famous skyline, is commemorated and immortalised in every medium known to man. So a shop full of souvenirs begins to resemble a kind of novelty graveyard, where the headstones take the form of baseball caps and wipe-clean tablemats. And aside from their morbid fascination with a scene of mass murder, these shops also reflect a wider issue, prevalent throughout the city and its people. New York is in denial. No one looks up anymore. No one wants to open their eyes and see the invisible proof of the towers' demise. For this reason, it is impossible to buy a picture of the revised Manhattan skyline. The only images available, be they on a T-shirt or a jam jar, make false promises about modern New York. If you came here in a time machine from September 10th 2001, no one would ever tell you the truth.

The conscienceless capitalists were out in force as we approached the proof of modern history's defining moment. Little tables lined the nearby streets, selling postcards, paintings and photographs of the most gruesome moments of the 9/11 tragedy. The people out there couldn't afford to be in denial – there was simply too much profit to be made from the truth. Among the most tasteless pieces of merchandise on offer was an Osama bin Laden toilet roll: his notorious face stamped with the legend 'Wipe Out Terrorism'.

As we got closer to the devastation, we walked alongside a wall lined with flowers and messages, sent or pinned there from far-flung destinations around the world. In among the generic offerings were personal shrines: photos and flowers for one or other of the four thousand dead. 'John, we miss you.' 'Gary, we love you.' 'Jane, you'll live on forever.' The street of remembrance was packed with onlookers, rubberneckers, well-wishers and disbelieving natives. Yet somehow, this massed crowd made no sound as it trudged unhurriedly along. And through opening my own mouth I quickly learned that the area had become a vacuum – where any attempted speech is stolen from the lips before it has a chance to punctuate the prevailing silence.

Turning the corner into further fields of recollection, where weathered American flags littered the walls like patriotic graffiti, I noticed a little Catholic church, where rescue workers (unaware, perhaps, of that title's futility) were being fed and looked after. At the entrance, greeting passing members of the crowd with a simple upturned palm, stood a priest, smiling in defiance. As we drew closer to him, I realised that he'd learned how to conquer the vacuum; that he'd regained the power to speak and make quiet sound. Passers-by seemed to find some crumb of comfort from his gentle words, looking expectantly up at him for wisdom. A little further along, young women held Christian leaflets outstretched with unsure smiles. Around the next corner, a giant cloth of red, white and blue, of stars and stripes, screamed GOD BLESS AMERICA. All around, in this unearthly place, the sense of religion was so strong that it could be touched and tasted.

Arthur shook his giant old head. Jacqui stayed close. One last turn of one further corner would provide the moment of truth. And as we approached it, the news footage began to play again. The planes, the dust, the screams to a hitherto unimportant God.

Around the final corner was a large building site, surrounded by high fences and portable work cabins which stood obstinately like bricks between us and the open wound. Put simply, there was nothing to see here, folks. Eight months of intensive clearing work had reduced the rubble to ground level and, as a result, if you couldn't see over the intentional barriers, you couldn't see anything. New York City had raised its proverbial middle finger to anyone who thought they were coming here to see a tourist attraction. On one edge of the site (which seemed ridiculously small; about the size of an out of town supermarket and car park), a viewing platform for relatives gave a better vantage point, although thankfully, none of us had the qualifications to access it. On the other side, a more gently-inclined public platform offered little more of a view than we had on the ground, and we certainly didn't have time to wait in the great winding queue for that. As a result, we soon turned and made for the hotel, relieved in some way to at least have stood at the site of the turning point of modern culture.

But before we did turn to leave, there was one thing to look at. Rising out of the middle of the site, and gleaming nakedly in the hot sun above the perimeter fence, was a giant metal cross. It was brown, rusted and beaten, and had been found amongst the rubble on the first terrible days of excavation. It had survived while everything else had disintegrated around it, and now it stood proudly alone, with all its fellow debris stripped and shipped away. A symbol of hope which few seemed to understand but from which all who saw it drew warmth. For

Arthur, it felt like a justification for Tough Talk's very presence in New York. There's a famous line in the Bible: 'The light shines in the darkness, and the darkness has not overcome it.' It seemed to me at that moment that a truer word has never been written. God is found amongst the dirt, amongst the dying and the desperate. It's reflected in the way Jesus mixed with the prostitutes and tax collectors of His time, and it's reflected in the way that a group of Englishmen travelled 'free and a 'arf fousand miles' to bring hope to a wounded city.

* * *

It'd been a hard and eventful day. We'd hardly relaxed since we'd arrived in the city, and Saturday evening presented perhaps the best opportunity for us to sample some authentic New York nightlife. Steve, Adam, Paul and I agreed to meet at eight for a lonely man's night out.

For two hours prior to that meeting however, I snatched at the chance to spend a little time in the horizontal position. Jet lag had been scrambling my head and destabilising my step since I'd arrived, and things were starting to get worse, not better. Despite my best attempts to persuade my brain that it was only 6 p.m., it argued stubbornly the cause for 11 p.m. I was shattered, but the idea of wasting a whole evening during this flying visit seemed unacceptable to me. I still wanted to see New York by night, with its neon illuminations and strange nocturnal beasts, and I wasn't about to let a little thing like jet lag get in my way. In the interest of sanity and avoiding collapse, I made a compromise with my body. I would lie down for an hour, but I wouldn't go to sleep. So all I needed now was a bit of half-decent American television to keep me awake.

TV in New York (and I'm assuming, the whole of the surrounding country) is dominated, not punctuated, by advertisements. And from what I saw, they're often a lot more entertaining than the shows around them. Take for example the wit of one subtle-as-a-chainsaw prime-time offering: two men sitting in a baseball dugout, waiting to go out to bat. One turns to the other and says, 'Hey buddy, do you want to hit a home run?' His friend turns back with an excited grin, and with an elegant, intelligent voice reminiscent of Pluto the dog, says 'Well I sure do!' Baseball player one hands him a small package and winks at camera. It's an advert, of course, for Viagra.

Unfortunately, it's not all as superb as that. Before I'd stumbled upon my chosen channel, I'd forced Paul to sit through three minutes of a Japanese cartoon, a flicker of a Spanish-language cookery show and a couple of bad gags from an American rewrite of a British sitcom which was lame enough even before the translation. But then, much to the delight of both of us, I found something – a link between US and UK culture and a Saturday night ratings-winner on either side of the Atlantic. There was no Cilla Black, but the name was the same. Perhaps people all over the world watch *Blind Date* as they're getting ready to go out.

The American *Blind Date* is very different to its British cousin. For a start, all the action revolves around a film of the date in question, rather than a studio with an audience on laughing gas. Contestants don't choose each other, but are instead thrown together very deliberately. And while Cilla's cheap, chirpy and cheerful version is all about slight innuendo and stolen kisses, the emphasis across the pond is slightly different. The edition of US *Blind Date* which robbed half an hour of my precious Saturday night aimed to put two people in bed together as quickly as possible, whilst 'accidentally' catching as much naked flesh on camera as possible.

Modern America is therefore a very confused place. On the one hand, it has a thriving Christian industry, a Christian music chart, and superchurches full of beautiful teenagers with 'True Love Waits' promise cards in their wallets. Its citizens pray daily, even if only when asking God to bless their nation, and its early morning political shows feel comfortable with discussing the God of the Bible and how He chooses to show favour. On the other hand, it mass-consumes popular early-evening TV shows about sexual promiscuity, it practically invented gun crime, and houses dubious delicatessens which its police allow to remain open to vend drugs and donuts in equal measure.

Switching off *Blind Date*, as yet another bikini burst unexpectedly open, Paul and I donned shirts and boots and headed into the night air. Out of the frying pan, and into the fire.

My best friend at University was a shaven-headed pit-bull-man who picked up the nickname 'Baz' for no good reason. In the summer before we met, he'd spent two months in the States with Camp America, and enjoyed a variety of experiences which then informed almost every conversation we had for the next four years. 'When I was in America . . . ' he would begin, like a soldier relating his wartime experiences, before going on to tell some anecdote or other. It seemed that in two months, this country had provided him with enough strange cultural experiences to feed a lifetime of storytelling. One of his favourite stories was: 'When I was in America, I had this thing called a Philly Cheese-steak Sandwich.' He'd tell it whenever we were in a hamburger joint, or walking back late at night with a kebab, in order to denigrate the food that we were then consuming. 'It was the nicest thing I've ever eaten' he would brag. 'You've got to have one if you ever go there.' I had no idea what a Philly Cheese-steak Sandwich was, but a hundred and fifty tellings of the story were enough to convince me that I wanted one real bad.

Strangely, we hadn't manage to eat since breakfast, and so first priority on our big night out was to replenish the boys' dangerously low food levels. Being the kind of men who bypass their taste buds when eating anyway, they were happy for me to choose the venue. This, I quickly realised, was my chance to fulfil Baz's commandment. In our many conversations on the subject, Baz had always made out that these things were as easy to get hold of in New York as a gram of cocaine. Sadly, this proved to be false information: every menu in every window appeared to suffer from a glaring omission in the sand-wich department. And despite the fact that every other establishment on our part of Broadway was either an eatery or a lapdancing club, a five-minute hunt reaped no dividends. Eventually, with dejection in my eyes, I settled for a fried chicken restaurant.

For the second time that day, I found myself sitting opposite Steve Johnson. Now if Paul could put food away, then Steve positively demolished the stuff. Conversation was completely impossible for the first three and a half minutes of the meal, as he ripped through his Chicken Combo with Fries like a starving sumo wrestler. Then, after a sip of cola and a gentle burp, he was ready to talk. I had just finished buttering my bread roll.

'I thought you were very good this morning,' I said genuinely.

'Did you fink so?' he bubbled. 'I fought it was a good meetin' generally.'

'Yes, you were all good.'

'Yes.'

'Mmm.'

I bit hard into my first piece of chicken and looked up at Steve as he drained his cup. Surely we – an ex-football referee and an ex-football hooligan – had absolutely nothing in common.

'You still missing your family?' I asked helpfully, pouring as much salt as I could into the bloody cut in his heart.

'Yes, I really miss 'em. Did I tell you what an angel my missus is?'

'You did. Tell me more.' I had to let him talk – I had too much ground to make up in the chicken stakes.

'Sometimes I look at her an' I don't know why she stuck wiv me. She's beautiful, my wife, looks like that bird off of *Wheel of Fortune*. When I was at my worst, I used to leave 'er at 'ome, up in a stinkin' tower block on 'er own wiv young kids, while I went off an' did what I wanted, spent all our money an' drank as much as possible. I'd disappear on a Friday, turn my mobile phone off, and then re-emerge from nowhere again on a Sunday afternoon.'

'Nice bloke,' I said, then wondered if I should have been that familiar with a man of eighteen stone. He smiled and nodded.

'Yes, I know. That's why I sometimes can't believe 'ow she stuck wiv me.' His brow furrowed briefly: 'I never 'it her you know. I never laid a finger on 'er, and perhaps that's why she stayed there. But it was the neglect, that's 'ow I really 'urt 'er.'

It reminded me somewhat of Jacqui's story.

'How did it affect your kids?' I was developing an unwanted journalistic knack for asking nasty private questions here.

'I can't really explain that one either. They've both turned out good as gold. Suppose it shows you what a good mother she's been to 'em, 'cause I wasn't around much. There was a time when I didn't care you know. I didn't care about anyone but me. I miss 'em terribly now though mate.'

Steve looked as if he was ready to sob into his napkin. As I finally finished my chicken, fifteen minutes after him, I tried to comprehend this unlikely person sitting opposite me. A hardened criminal, fuelled by alcohol and a love for violence, transformed into a family man ready to weep for the family he'd left behind. If anyone in the world epitomised a changed man, it was him. And although in these cynical times it's easy for words – especially the J-word – to lose their impact and meaning, it was now crystal clear to me why, when he pointed the way to Jesus Christ, it had such a powerful effect. It wasn't his size or his muscles that were impressive to people, nor was it the terrible story of violence and alcohol that he called his early life. It was the man who now stood before people, who could tell those stories but then stand as a testament to the force that miraculously changed and saved him – that's what made him   incredible.

On the other table, Adam and Paul puffed impatiently as I swigged at the last dregs of my drink. Jet lag was beginning to work its magic in their heads too, proving that there's an arrogance in the British man which simply refuses to conform to any other time zone outside of Greenwich. (This was later proven further by Steve's admission that he hadn't bothered to reset his watch.) Leaving the chicken coop, we were confronted by a multitude of multicoloured neon – a sea of signs that all demanded we followed their recommendations. But we were tired, and wilted through the doors of the first bar we could find. In pumping New York nightlife terms, this proved to be a bum steer to end all others.

'My name is Zola, I'm from Outer Mongolia' said the girl, with words that could have been lifted from a bad song lyric.

We'd somehow stumbled into the worst bar in the whole world. The beer was twice as expensive as it was anywhere else in the city, and there were only five people apart from ourselves in there at nine o'clock on a Saturday night. In the middle of the room danced Zola, a drunk Asian girl of no more than twenty-two. Behind the bar, trapped like a fly in a jar by the contract of her employment, was a particularly bored-looking waitress. Lodged in the doorway and preventing a draught was a huge bouncer with a gold tooth. And positioned as far from each other as possible, at opposite ends of the bar, sat a transvestite and a very dodgy-looking African-American with hand permanently in pocket. Only jet lag demanded that we didn't put up a fight for our evening. We sat quietly down as eight eyes watched, and Zola crashed into us.

Paul, Adam and I laughed as Steve fired off a series of jokes about the décor. The girl behind the bar was less than impressed, and demanded that we buy some drinks. We obliged, and she left us alone. The same could not be said for the dancing girl, the transvestite and the African-American, who were probably as inquisitive about why three big blokes in matching jackets and a limp little boy had wandered into their rarely-frequented hideout as we were about them.

The dancing girl staggered over and introduced herself. She was depressed, she told us through a thick accent, in one of a series of incoherent statements. She was a student of social work at a New York university, and on Saturday night she had no friends to party with. She missed her boyfriend, who was back in Mongolia, and she'd wandered in here because it was empty and she could dance. Then, without asking us any questions, she floated back to the dance floor for Abba's 'Dancing Queen'. Shrugging off the bizarreness of the evening so far, Paul and Adam attempted to engage the rap-star lookalike in the corner in conversation, and Steve and I picked up from where we'd left off in the Chicken emporium.

'You know, for the first two years that we were to-gever,' confessed Steve, 'my wife didn't even know my real name.'

'What?' I nearly lost a mouthful of beer at this admission. I'd heard of relationships built on deceit, but this was ridiculous. 'What did she think your name was?'

'Jones,' he giggled in a manner you wouldn't expect for a man with his face. 'It was the first fing that came into my 'ead.'

'Your girlfriend thought your name was Steve Jones for two years? Why?'

'Because I didn't want her knowin' fings abaat me. I wanted to be in control of everyone an' everyfing.'

'When did you tell her the truth?'

'Just before we signed the marriage register.'

'Dancing Queen' had finished; Zola was on her way back. It seemed like a good moment to take a trip to the toilet.

On my return, everyone in the bar, except Zola, was grinning or holding back laughter. As I approached my stool, she was already lurching towards me, with a pen in one hand and a napkin in the other.

'Please!' she yelped with unbridled excitement. 'Please! Sign autograph for me!'

I had clearly been stitched up here. In the ninety seconds of my absence, they'd told her that I was a famous journalist from the BBC.

'Go on mate,' shouted Adam behind her. 'Sign her an autograph so she can show her friends.'

I looked up at Steve for an explanation. He caved in almost instantly, convinced by the hilarity of his own joke.

'I've just been tellin' Zola 'ere abaat what we all do for a livin'.'

'Oh really?' I replied with eyebrow raised. 'Could you just remind me what that is?'

Paul butted in: 'You know mate – Steve here is a body-guard.'

'Oh.' That wasn't very imaginative, I thought.

'For the Queen.'

'Ah.'

Adam took up the baton. 'Paul here, as you know, is the drummer from the Rolling Stones.'

'Charlie Watts?' I asked in a high-pitched, incredulous tone.

'That's me!' said Paul, the distinguished actor.

The barriers erected by alcohol and language were preventing Zola from cottoning on to the joke, even when Steve explained that Adam was the most famous toilet cleaner in all of Old London Town, and that all three of them knew the Queen and Tony Blair person-ally.

'And you're a famous BBC journalist, aren't you mate?' they chirped in unison.

'Please sign autograph!' Zola's persistence was matched only by her ability to dance badly.

I gave up. I took the pen and the napkin and scribbled a message. And as she trotted off, I hoped two things. First, that she'd be pleased tomorrow when she discov-ered that she had Sir Trevor McDonald's autograph, and second, that she'd never get the opportunity to watch *News at Ten*.

We left the bar just before eleven, while our body clocks told us that we'd just left a club. For the information of the liberal among you, we'd had a couple of watered-down American beers each, and for the puritanical among you, we'd kept it to a couple. And as we wandered home, as sober as a judicial convention but inebriated by laughter, I took a long look at my new friends. Three Christian men who knew how to balance real life and real faith, who knew how to have fun, but also where to draw the line. I felt for the first time in my life, walking down one of the worldliest streets in the world, that this kind of balancing act, that Christians have been failing at for centuries, was actually possible. It is possible to live in a fallen world, and not get sucked into falling down with it, without running off into a Christian cubby-hole and hiding there until the rapture. It's a tightrope, and it's hard, but it is possible. And unless the church is prepared to walk that tightrope – to engage with the culture instead of condemning it, then people like Tough Talk are fighting a losing battle.

Chapter 8

A Tough Message

Sunday morning, 6.05 a.m., and I'm at Times Square again. And suddenly, I'm Tom Cruise, and I work out when they must have filmed that bit in *Vanilla Sky*.

This was always going to be the most gruelling day of the mission. Tough Talk were booked to speak at three consecutive services at a church in the Bronx, covering the hours between nine in the morning and three in the afternoon. Food over that time was going to be at a minimum and, therefore, the horrified consensus was that we'd have to get up with the birds and the builders and stock up with a hearty breakfast. So even at this unsociable hour, we'd scattered ourselves around early-morning New York like a pack of mercenaries on the hunt for treasure. And undeterred by my failure on the previous evening, I was determined to fulfil Baz's demand and find myself a Philly Cheese-steak Sandwich.

Walking along an emptier, but no less commercial Broadway, I was stopped suddenly by the quiet cry of a small, huddled figure, who appeared to have spent the night lying in front of the theatre where they film David Letterman's *Late Show*.

'Got a dime sir?' yawned the haggard little man, with what were possibly his first words of the day.

To be honest, and entirely ignorant, I was not sure what a 'dime' was. I certainly didn't have in my possession a small chocolate-covered caramel bar, but I had a feeling that I was barking up the wrong tree there.

'I have some dollars and cents', I replied without thinking.

His thin face lit up and I saw it properly for the first time. He was a particularly harmless-looking homeless man, with grubby black skin, a surprisingly well-groomed beard and the donated clothes of a fat white man. A couple of fuzzy hair curls were escaping from his holey hat, and the worldly possessions on which he was perched barely filled two shopping bags.

'Here's a couple of dollars' I said, because I could say nothing else. Then I smiled, dropped my head, and began to walk away.

'Where are you from buddy?' asked the voice behind me. I turned. This wasn't part of the deal, surely? I would have thought that he'd have lots of things to be getting on with, rather than talking to me. He had made his sale already, after all.

'London.'

'London!' his whole body lurched into a new animated state at the very mention of the word, like a Disney video that's been switched from pause to play. 'I know London! I played Jazz in London in '69!'

I nodded insincerely.

'You like Jazz, brother? I know you English people like Jazz.'

I nodded again, insincerely again. Where was he going with this?

'You need to get down to Small's my friend. Greenwich Village. Yes sir – best joint in New York City.'

Suddenly my insincerity melted. Suddenly I did care about Jazz – there was a melody in his voice that convinced me that I did, even though I didn't. His words themselves were like music, in a strange way: like the sudden improvisational bursts of the jazzman. I couldn't help it – I liked this man; this man was cool. He didn't deserve to be there out at the front of the theatre. With a different set of circumstances, maybe he'd be in Letterman's band.

I took down the directions, and as a matter of courtesy, paid out a couple more dollars. Then I thanked him and went on my way. But I turned back once again, struck by an idea. Perhaps, I thought, this was the modern equivalent of that shoeshine boy from *Police Squad* – perhaps this was the man with his ear to the ground – the informant to the whole city . . .

'You don't know where I could get a Philly Cheesesteak Sandwich do you?' asked my overhanging gut.

The little hobo sucked his teeth. 'Now there is a question buddy. I know where you can get a fine steak sandwich. I know where I can get you a steak sandwich with cheese. But I'm sorry, I don't know one place in this city that will cook you up a Philly. I'm just beat.'

My heart sank. It looked as if I would have to return home without experiencing this supposed eighth wonder of the world. Baz would never forgive me. I thanked the homeless man again, and this time managed to drag myself from his gravity. My stomach rumbled – stretched by two and a bit days in the fat man's paradise – and my sense of culinary adventure sucked me into the very next, exotic, restaurant.

When I left McDonalds, twenty minutes later, my friend was still attempting to hook his next duck. The streets were beginning to busy again now, but the natives had no interest in stopping to talk. I had a little time to kill before I was expected to meet the others, and so squatted back down to join him again. After all, you can learn a lot about a city from its homeless people.

'It's you again! The Philly Cheese-brother! Hey, and you've been fed. What you drinking, buddy?'

'Root beer.' This was another concession to Baz – the fact that McDonalds in the US still serves root beer was also a source of constant excitement to him throughout our university years.

'That's a big root beer,' said the jazzman. 'Did you know buddy, that root beer is a strong laxative. You don't want to go drinking too much of that.' (The inherent correctness of this assertion relates to a later story, the details of which shall not, fortunately, be divulged here.)

'They don't do root beer in London,' I burped. 'I go back tomorrow, so it's my last chance.'

'You go back tomorrow? How long you been here?'

'Couple of days, just a flying visit really.'

'You been sightseeing? You seen Ground Zero?' His eyes suddenly narrowed.

'I went there yesterday. It was horrible. You?'

'I've never been, and Buddy, you'd never get me there. I tell you, this city ain't the same this year, and that's the reason. People don't smile any more, people don't use their wallets any more – and as you can imagine, for me that's a problem.' His face had switched now – as if a light switch had just been flicked inside his head – from happy-go-lucky to downbeat deadbeat. The emotional drain of the last few months was tragically plain to see, even in a man who'd be forgiven for refusing to smile.

'Well . . . I'm just so sorry . . . about what happened.' My words were lame and feeble and I knew it. I paused and looked at the floor; it was time to make my excuses. 'I guess I'd better be going now . . . er . . . ' I didn't know his name.

'It's okay buddy,' he said, looking beyond me. 'My name's Elijah.'

'Elijah,' I repeated thoughtfully, and the recognition of his existence made him smile. For a moment I stared into space too. Maybe I'd been around evangelists for too long, but I could see how this could turn into an evangelistic opportunity. His name is taken from the Bible – that's a starting point. Then I could ask him what he thought about the Bible. Then I could tell him what I thought about the Bible. Then I could preach at him for a while, and nab his homeless little soul . . .

'Goodbye Elijah,' I said instead, and headed back to the hotel, thankful that I hadn't acted on my ridiculous impulse. Being a Christian is not all about scalping as many souls as possible. It's about love. Elijah needed food, a shelter, a conversation that made him feel human. I was able to help him a little bit with some of that and, thank God, I didn't go and spoil it by hitting him with a Bible.

* * *

'Bronx? Twenny minutes, no problem'

The door of the Lincoln slammed again. Shockingly, Dario heaved it open again exactly twenty minutes later.

'See?' he laughed, revealing at last that he'd been in on the joke all along. 'Twenny minutes!'

Crossroads Tabernacle, the Bronx-based church at the end of our twenny-minute rainbow, appeared from the outside to have a lot in common with its cousin across the city. Again we had parked up outside a large, windowless building not unlike an old cinema, which encroached on the street by virtue of a large flat-roofed canopy labelled with 'Jesus Saves', or something similar. Again, we were standing in one of the world's most notorious neighbourhoods. And again, there were big-hearted friendly-faced people waiting at the entrance, just falling over themselves to welcome us inside.

A quick stroll through the box-office doors (and past where the popcorn should have been) took us into a sanctuary which bore more of a resemblance to the Tyseley Health and Fitness Centre than it did to the first church we'd visited. If someone had told me that an explosion had recently been detonated in this room, I could have quite believed them. A work in progress, with ambitious refurbishment plans underway but by no means completed, it was a great white expanse of unfinished plaster and temporary measures. The back half of the room was completely out of use and the vast stage at the front was a shapeless black hole that lacked a feeling of safety. The proudly displayed plans were a thing for the future – right now this place looked like a half-cleared bombsite.

A larger-than-life steward made his way towards Ian, who was still wiping the sleep from his eyes. His badge told us that he was Richard, and his mouth told us that we were welcome. He showed us to the front of the church, where Tough Talk would be performing, and then begged our patience in waiting for the weights, which were being transported across from Queens. As we waited, various members of what appeared to be a full gospel choir began to encircle us with curious eyes. They had heard us talking, and had been transfixed by our accents (apart from Steve's, which they assumed to be Australian). Soon the questioning began – 'do you know Prince William?' and the like. As this was a church, I decided against impersonating another newsreader.

Pastor Joseph Cortese introduced himself shortly before the nine o'clock service was due to begin. He was a different proposition to Pastor Adam: quieter, more slightly built, and with a prayer style that more closely resembled what the more conservative among us might call 'normal'. He too was intensely excited to welcome Tough Talk (and not the Power House Team this time) to his humble church, and made the point very clearly when introducing them on stage moments later.

'Can I ask all the 'blokes' in here to stand up please?' exclaimed Pastor Cortese with gusto.

Thoughtlessly, the male members of our party, myself included, rose to our feet – the only men to do so in a 400-strong audience. The earlybird congregation began to laugh. We sat.

'These guys have come all the way from London to be with us this morning. Now I was talking to them before-hand and they told me that 'bloke' is the London word for a man.' Cortese chuckled, inducing further uproar. 'Alright, now can I ask all the 'birds' to stand up please?' A few bright-spark ladies stood and smirked.

'A bird is the London slang for a woman, I believe.' Even more uncontrollable guffawing followed. It became clear that Cortese was not a conventional pastor, who'd introduce the songs, say a solemn prayer or two, and bless everyone. No, Cortese was a lot more your Jerry Seinfeld type.

'Can you believe that?' he asked, gesticulating wildly. Incredulous giggling arose.

'Birds and blokes!' Sides were splitting left, right and centre. The sixteen Londoners on the front row smiled politely.

I wasn't entirely won over by the routine (although I was later informed that an understanding of Bronx street language would have made it a lot funnier), but Cortese was certainly a good warm-up man. By the time Arthur got up to lead the boys on stage, the early crowd were wide awake and full of smiles.

'Good morning Crossroads Tabernacle!' shouted Arthur above the trademark music, and grinning more than usual. 'We're a bunch of ordinary men, but we serve an extraordinary God. His name is Jesus Christ. Come on!'

And off we went again.

This time, something was wrong. It may have been early, but Arthur's usual coherence was missing as he told his story. Whole chunks of his life were brushed over, while others were repeated three times. He was addicted to cocaine. Then Jesus saved his life. Then he had an adulterous affair. This was not the polished testimony I'd heard him give so many times before. This was the B-side – a remixed version that had been cobbled together by some two-bit DJ. And although alarm bells were beginning to ring inside my head, Arthur seemed unconcerned. In his mind at least, everything was going swimmingly.

Steve's story also suffered from similar inconsistencies. The jokes were missing their target for the first time, and it was clear that his accent was causing problems for the listening congregation. I started to get a sinking feeling, and a nervous glance from Jacqui told me that I wasn't alone. What was going on?

After Steve's initial ramble came to an end, Arthur was involved again, this time deadlifting a piffling starter weight. The look on his face as he took the strain was enough to tell me that things were about to go from bad to worse. He was puffing and reddening as if he was attempting to break the world record. Sweat was rolling down his forehead. For an awful moment I wondered if he'd even manage it. Finally, with enormous and

unusual effort, he managed to separate the two hundred-
pound bar from the ground.

Steve continued to lack focus and direction, and
Arthur continued to bust a gut with every lift. And as
this lacklustre display continued, I tried desperately but
without inspiration to work out what was wrong. Half
an hour later, after Ian had wrapped up with all the neat-
ness of a fine artist in gardening gloves, a usually quiet
member of the Tough Talk spiritual 'pit team' piped up
with their thoughts:

'I don't normally say things like this,' said the tyre-
changer to the refueller, 'but I really felt that God was
speaking to me during that meeting. I felt that there was
something wrong in everyone's attitude. I think they
were speaking with their own words and lifting with
their own strength.'

On the face of it, this prophecy seemed to lack something in the insight department. What else were they
going to speak and lift with? But that wasn't what was
meant. The feeling was that, for once, Tough Talk had
walked out on stage without their most important member: the man upstairs. That's not to say that their
watered-down message had no effect. There were still
around forty commitments made after Ian's appeal –
proof positive that God can use people despite themselves. But the show simply wasn't as good as it had been
before – it wasn't the paint-blistering display of strength
and spirit that had been put on in Queens twenty-four
hours earlier. And although I had begun to believe that
these men were almost capable of doing no wrong, I had
to admit that bad attitude sounded like a good explanation.

'We felt,' chirped the tyre-changer and the refueller in
nervous unison, 'that there was something wrong with
that . . . it wasn't quite right.'

'You're telling me,' Arthur nodded solemnly. 'That first bar was just over two hundred pounds and it felt like a ton.'

'We thought that it would be a good idea if everyone gathered together to pray before the next service,' said the tyre-changer, gathering confidence. 'Maybe we could pray for you – that is why we came out here after all.'

Arthur nodded again, and sixteen Londoners disappeared backstage.

At the makeshift front-of-stage, the gospel choir warmed up for the 11 o'clock service. As they did so, somewhere through a network of corridors behind them, Tough Talk were surrounded by their prayer support group. There had been a general admission made that the first performance had lacked focus and inspiration, and now everyone was praying hard that Act II would not provide a repeat performance. There were prayers for wisdom, prayers for humility and prayers for strength. In the midst of the huddle, one of the lifters began to cry. The prayers grew more intense, more heartfelt, more desperate. The praise songs of the choir began to ring around the building and echo through every soul. For a few seconds the atmosphere was so thick with emotion that it was impossible to release any more. Then quietness descended, and along with it came a much-needed sense of peace. The tears dried, the hugs began to flow. They were ready for the second round, and this time, they meant business.

I watched a rejuvenated Arthur as he wowed the second congregation with his storytelling delivery. The transformation that had taken place was almost indescribable. When he spoke about his affair and mentioned, as he always did, that his wife was here with him today, I was moved to tears. And as I pretended that I had something in my eye, I wondered how a story I'd heard ten times before could possibly have such an effect on me.

Steve also produced a complete return to form. His comic timing had been completely restored, his stories had regained their edge. The audience, far from being lost this time in a cloud of glottal stops, were now hanging on his every word. And in the powerlifting breaks, Arthur was shifting weight like a human ant. Adam and Gordon, previously a little sloppy with their weight changing and equipment moving, had suddenly regained military discipline.

And then, after two life stories had been perfectly told, Ian looked out and saw four hundred pairs of mesmerised eyes staring back at him. Unlike the mainly-Christian early audience, he was now getting ready to address a far more mixed bunch. Again, there were some pretty bad people in a few of those seats – this was the Bronx after all. But they had heard stories that echoed their own, and they had heard of how men had escaped from those seemingly inescapable destinies through Jesus Christ. And now they wanted to know how they could get in on the deal. You could sense it just by looking out across the half-built hall at those faces. They wanted to buy the product – they just needed to know the freephone number. And who better to tell it to them than shopping-channel McDowall?

'I want to reiterate what the others have already said,' began Ian. 'We don't tell you any of these stories to try to glorify ourselves – I am deeply ashamed of many of the things I've done.'

All along the front of the stage, the Tough Talkers had fanned themselves out into a straight line, so that they looked like a group of overgrown Cub Scouts on parade. Behind Ian, every pair of evangelists' eyes stared straight ahead, as if they were all focused on a point far in the distance. Importantly, the end result was that they looked serious, and that gave an added authority to Ian's words.

'But I want to tell you,' he continued, 'that Jesus Christ saved my life. And sometimes you need to let some stories come out so that people can know the power that took you out of that lifestyle.'

In the Cub Scout line, Arthur and Steve both took brief glances at the floor as Ian uttered those words. It was clear that they weren't proud of their stories either.

'I haven't got time to tell you the whole of my story this morning, but I want to tell you this part of it. One night I was involved in a fight – I was working as a doorman, so it happened a lot. And this particular night the fight spilled out onto the . . . well, I'd call it the pavement, but it's a sidewalk here isn't it? This fight was what I would call 'kicking off' – everyone was fighting hard, and mean and dirty. It was madness – mayhem – with bodies and fists everywhere. I started to get hit, and I began to panic.'

If this had been Brighton, Bristol or Brentford, there might have been a few gasps at this point in Ian's tale. But this was the Bronx, and the only response came in the slow nodding of heads.

'Now I used to carry with me a knuckle-duster – I believe the term used here is a 'brass knuckle.' At the end of this thing was a stabbing object, and on this particular evening, I remember pulling out my knuckle-duster as I was being hit; I remember sticking the spikes in a guy's face; I remember twisting the thing round, and stabbing him. I remember jumping on his head.'

The nods gained vigour. Ian's volume increased sharply.

'The Bible says "the soul that sins descends into utter hell." That evening, as I drove home, I felt an ugliness

grip hold of my heart. I felt a darkness inside me. I'd
crossed to another level, if you understand what I mean.
And something inside me – inside my consciousness –
was hardened. My feelings got hard that night. I had a
heart of stone. I didn't care what I did, and who I did it
to. My life started to go down in a spiral, and hatred, fear,
paranoia and anger seemed to follow me wherever I
went. I used to go to bed with a carving knife under the
pillow. I wouldn't go out of the house without having
weapons on me. When you get followed home and
pulled over by people who say they're going to shoot
you, when you find yourself getting arrested and getting
involved in attacks, you kind of go down a path. Maybe
you can't understand why you're going that way, but it's
a path of darkness. Well the Bible says that there's a way
that seems right to man, but it's path leads to death and
destruction.'

These quotes from the Bible were keeping the more
respectable section of the audience interested. But they
were drawing a good response from the other element
too, as were the references to getting arrested and the use
of weapons.

'Death was something I feared: I had a fear of being
stabbed and shot. I had a fear of dying. But one night,
without giving you the rest of the story, after breaking up
a fight and driving home from the club, I had a gun in the
boot of the car, I had a policeman's truncheon – a bat –
under the seat, I had a brass knuckle in my pocket, blood
on my shirt and I was waiting to go to court on a charge
of violence and disorder – which carries up to five years
imprisonment. That evening, I called out to God.'

It had struck me many times before, but it never felt
more poignant than at this particular moment. A group
of former hardmen from East London, their lives radic-
ally changed by life-saving encounters with God, had

come out here to Queens and the Bronx to tell their stories to the hard and hardened men and women of America. That in itself was a pretty amazing story, but it wasn't the most spectacular thing of all. The most spectacular thing of all was that not only did these London boys speak, but also, the people of New York listened. It happened on the streets; it happened at breakfast with the men; and in the evening with the gang kids. It was happening now. Ian related how he'd called out to God, and a room full of people from the other side of the world, but the same part of life, got ready to do the same.

'I called out to Jesus Christ,' continued Ian loudly, 'because I remembered something that someone once said to me. He said, "Ian, everyone has fallen short of God's standards." He said "It doesn't matter who you are – everyone has broken God's standards." And this particular night, for the first time ever, I felt guilty for what I had just done. Now I'd been working as a night-club bouncer and doorman for ten years, breaking up five to seven fights a night. Violence and bloodshed were normal for me. But that evening, I was talking to myself about God, without ever really going to a church or knowing a Christian. I felt guilty for what had happened, and for the way I was living. I said "God, if you're real, what would you make of somebody like me? God, if you're real, could you forgive someone like me?" And I felt a love saturate my heart. My heart of stone turned into flesh, and God poured His Spirit into me. I felt this love touch me, and I cried my eyes out. That evening, something happened to me that the other guys have already talked about: I was "born again". I never knew anything about church. But I knew and could not deny that Jesus Christ was alive.

'I went to a church in a place called Canning Town, East London, which is the kind of area where you can't

get car insurance, where they put padlocks on the dust-
bins. It's a bit rough, and it's where I grew up. I went into
this church, and they were there clapping, and making a
big noise, and I was shocked – I didn't know what was
going on. I sat there with dark sunglasses on, trying to
hide the bruising from a fight I'd had the night before. I
was weighing seventeen stone and I sat there in this
church, at the back, and my heart was crying out to God.
I was involved in every form of crime that you could
imagine; I'd never had a job in my life, never worked a
nine-to-five. But Jesus Christ came into my life and something gripped hold of me.

'I started to read the Bible – you see I'd never even
picked up a Bible before. I'd left school without any edu-
cation, and I thought you had to be intelligent to be able
to read one of these things. I picked it up anyway, and I
was shocked that I could suddenly understand what was
in there, and I could read it. I could not deny what God
had done in my life. I could not deny that Jesus Christ
was real. And as I read the Bible, there were things in
there that shocked me. You see I thought that
Christianity was all about being good and nice, and all
pleasant things like that. When I started to read some of
the things that Jesus said, it shocked me.

'I read that Jesus said that in even calling your friend a
fool you are in danger of hellfire. I thought: my God, I've
been calling people a fool since I could speak. In my
house, swearing was a normal way of life. I grew up with
four brothers and two sisters – seven of us kids in a small
flat, and my baby brother's first word was a swear word.
I remember my grandmother coming over just before she
died, and she said to my mum, "What is it that Jason's
saying?" Jason had a nappy on, and he was running
around the flat saying this one word. And my mum was
so embarrassed that she had to lie. She said, "He's saying

ship, ship, ship!" That was normal behaviour in my life. And as I read the gospel, I realised that it was not normal in God's eyes.

'In fact, because of such behaviour, the wrath of God was upon mankind. I found that there was a curse upon the world. I found, as I looked into the scriptures, that the Bible said that man rebelled from God, that man fell short of God's standards. The Bible says that man sinned, and through his sin, death entered the world. And because all have sinned, all shall die. The Bible said that it has been appointed once for man to die, and then the judgement. "The wages of sin", it said, "are death". I found that actually what I thought was normal behaviour was not normal in God's eyes. I found that every man and every woman will be held accountable for such things, whether it's done in ignorance or not. And I've got to tell you that we call ourselves Tough Talk because this is a tough message. But I believe that this is the gospel of Jesus Christ.'

After this brief brush with fire and brimstone, Ian wrapped the meeting up in the usual way. A flautist began to play 'Amazing Grace' as he spoke, which had happened at the end of every event. He explained once more what being born again really meant, just as he had on Friday and Saturday. He asked everyone to bow their heads as he prayed, and asked those who agreed with the prayer to join him in saying 'Amen'. Again, this was just how it had been done before. He prayed and, as always, it was a simple prayer of repentance, of accepting Christ. And then, after the prayer, he asked the same question he always asked:

'If you've just prayed that prayer, while every head is still bowed, I'd ask you to just raise your hand.'

This crunch moment, which had featured at the end of every Tough Talk meeting on the mission, had always proved inspiring. Ian always insisted on acknowledging every raised hand – every saved soul – with a 'God bless you.' At the end of every meeting so far, this had therefore resulted in an almost constant repetition of those three words for at least twenty or thirty seconds as the hands went up. Each time we'd seen maybe forty or fifty commitments made, and Ian's quick-moving mouth had just been able to keep up.

But now he was beaten. The sheer volume of desperate reaching arms was too great. This time the number was much closer to a hundred. Perhaps a quarter of the room had decided to become Christians. Ian gave up, and after the first twenty repetitions greeted this new flock of believers into the faith simultaneously:

'God bless you all.'

The third meeting followed a similar pattern to the second. Arthur, Steve and Ian were all on top form, with the self-reliance of the early morning completely evaporated. Arthur even lifted his biggest weight of the whole mission, and that, after having had trouble with what was little more than a doorstop in the first meeting. There were fewer in attendance – as one might expect for a 1 p.m. service on a hot New York day – but once again, the crowd were won over by both the men and their faith. Another forty or so people were welcomed into Christianity, and the shell-shocked Pastor Cortese was moved to tears.

It was against the rules, but since it was the final meeting I seized the chance to turn around as these private commitments were made. The men and women in that room were showcasing the full emotional spectrum. Twenty-stone men with gold teeth were on their knees. Women and children of all shapes, sizes and colours were beaming with enlightenment. And in the back row, with both arms outstretched, a giant Hispanic man who had previously seen no need or place for religion, was now calling out to his God for the first time. My jaw dropped as I saw his face clearly – a face I'd seen many times before. It was our cab driver, Dario.

That day, nearly two hundred people from one of the hardest areas in America made a decision about their lives. They listened to stories of people who may have been from across the sea, but who they could relate to. They were persuaded by those stories that not only was there a God, but that somehow He was relevant to their lives today. And they had decided, *en masse*, to refocus their lives in His direction. In these cynical times, it's not the sort of story you hear every day.

Chapter 9

Back to Zero

The mission was over, completed, successful. Every meeting, from the street outreach to the back-to-back Bronx services, had paid dividends. Before we'd left London, Ian had told me that if one person had become a Christian as a result of the trip, the whole thing would have been worthwhile. They weren't keeping score, but it was a fact that after that one person did make a commitment to the faith, he or she was followed by nearly three hundred more. The potential impact that this one weekend could have on Queens and the Bronx was quite staggering. So now, at the end of the road, Ian and Co. were wearing thick smiles that came from thankful hearts.

After six straight hours of powerlifting, speaking and standing still, the members of Tough Talk could give no more. By early on Sunday evening, many of them had succumbed to a combination of physical exhaustion and still-prevalent jet lag and retired to their quarters. But, buoyed by several cups of strong coffee, I was determined to stick it out. After all, we'd be on a plane home within twelve hours, and it might be my last chance to see this incredible city for a while. I found an ally in

Adam McMillan, whose body clock had finally updated itself and synchronised with US time, just at the point at which this was no longer desirable. Together, we would be tourists just once more.

Before turning off his great drug-free engine for the night, Arthur put us in touch with a possible tour guide. Anna was a Puerto Rican police detective who had been initially involved in getting Tough Talk to revisit New York. Arthur called her on the off-chance that she might be off-duty, and to our good fortune she was. She agreed to give us a guided tour of her offices at the NYPD, and within an hour she had arrived at the hotel to pick us up.

'You been to this city befowre?' asked Anna in her seventies sitcom Brooklyn voice. She was a small, powerful-looking lady with well managed hair and fierce goggled eyes.

'First time' I replied from the passenger seat of her unusually small car.

'Then you never saw New York' she replied, her voice all sadness and regret. 'New York befowre 9/11 was a very different place to the New York you're looking at now.'

For the next twenty minutes, as we drove from Broadway to the Borough, her precinct, Anna spoke and I listened. Behind us, Adam shifted around uneasily, finding himself in the back of a police car for not the first time in his life.

Anna was putting on a brave face, but it was clear from all she told us and the way she told it, that she was one of the walking wounded. She'd lost friends and colleagues in the September 11th attacks, and she'd then spent the last nine months as part of the organisation charged with the responsibility of restoring normality and order. As an involved member both of Police Officers For Christ and Christ's Tabernacle, she'd found some solace in her faith, but she was still hurting terribly.

'You want some cawffee guys?' asked Anna as we sat around her desk, unsure as to why we'd been placed there.

'No thanks,' replied Adam for both of us.

'Then I'll just show you this.' Anna was being deliberately cryptic, building a little suspense as if we were children waiting for our Christmas presents. She was fumbling electronically, attempting to make her computer perform an operation despite its obvious reluctance to do so. Eventually, she managed to crack the code. Pushing us both closer to the screen and turning the machine's speakers up to full volume, she was proud to present what appeared at first to be an out-of-date photographic slideshow.

A picture of the World Trade Center, as it once was, flashed up onto the screen. It faded and was replaced with another, taken from a different angle but still showing no signs of harm. The speakers began to gurgle into life. Music had started to play, building slowly from a soft introduction. As it did so, some more famous pictures began to appear on screen. There were shots of Plane One hitting the first tower and of Plane Two looming into view. As the photographs became more recognisable, and their subject more severe, the music followed suit. Adam and I exchanged a look of recognition as we realised together that this was the music from the Old Spice adverts: the classical piece that unimaginative television programmes always use as a soundtrack accompaniment to scenes of death and destruction. As the slideshow continued, and the pictures became more and more vivid, not to mention memorable, I could sense a figure hopping nervously from foot to foot behind us. Anna was putting us through this – I knew not why – but she was putting herself through it too. In that empty darkened office, as the three of us relived the most monumental moments of modern history, I had the feeling that this slideshow was viewed with a tormenting regularity.

The electronic heart-mill lasted for a little more than ten minutes. As it threatened to loop around and start again, Anna pushed aside the shadows and encouraged us to get up and move on.

'The reason I showed you that,' she explained, at last, 'was that I'm going to get one of my friends to take you down to the site. I think he can actually get you inside Ground Zero.'

I was grateful to receive this news, as I had thought that my glance from afar on Saturday afternoon would be the closest I'd get. But I didn't quite see why we'd been forced to sit through this therapy session beforehand. It didn't matter. Five minutes later we were being introduced to the man who could open doors that would usually remain closed, and who would be responsible for another late night.

'Sergeant Val Suarez, at your service,' said the man in police uniform.

Anna bid us farewell, and Adam, Val and I exchanged brief life stories. It turned out that our newest friend was one of four sergeants who that night had been placed in control of the central NYPD command centre. Practically speaking, it would have been hard, on a Sunday evening, to find yourself in the company of a more influential police officer in that city. He was not the tallest man, but his stripes, service awards, gun and badge gave him a great deal of authority. His face bore a couple of slight scars, and his body had a peculiarly misshapen quality to it. When he walked, there was an odd kink in his movement. Like Anna, he considered himself a fully paid-up and born-again member of the Christian faith.

'What about Anna, eh?' exclaimed Val suddenly. 'What a great girl. She's like a sister to me. She's one of the good ones, you know.'

Adam and I nodded in unison, and he smiled.

'So you want to go to Ground Zero' he asked rhetorically. 'We can do that. You not seen it yet?'

'We went down there yesterday,' I explained, 'but we only stood at the side of the road. We couldn't get closer.'

'So you want to get closer? We can do that. Sure. No problem.' There was a positivity in Val's voice that was so pure, so full of life, that I suspected one could never grow tired of hearing it.

'Well, thanks. We didn't expect–'

'Hey,' he interrupted, 'as if struck by a brilliant idea. 'The station is only a couple of blocks down the way from here. Do you want to come and see inside the NYPD command centre?'

'Yeah!' Adam nearly jumped out of his seat as he snatched at Val's offer.

'Let's go down there first. I've got a couple of hours to kill right now; I can show you around. In fact, if you guys have got nowhere to be, we could hang out for a bit, and I could show you some more of the city.'

From nowhere, we suddenly had our own private tour guide. He had access to the whole city, he drove a big red BMW, and he had a gun on his hip. Could life get any better than this, I wondered, before chancing my arm.

'Val,' I said, still uncomfortable with the formulation of a sound that I had always assumed was short for Valerie. 'You don't know, by any chance, where I could get a Philly Cheese-steak Sandwich, do you?'

He nearly stopped the car in surprise at the question. He thought hard, running a full check on his in-head database of the city. His brow creased a little, then relaxed, shifting the skin on his face back and forth.

'I guess we could try the Village' he said after a while. 'They've got to do a Cheese-steak sandwich down there. They'll do you anything down there.'

I allowed myself a grin. Perhaps, even at the last opportunity, I was going to have my wish granted. Val quickly established an itinerary. We'd go to the NYPD first, to give him a chance to pick up some cash and gasoline, then we'd access all areas at Ground Zero. And then, if I was very lucky, we'd finally complete the quest for the Holy Grail.

Adam McMillan, former villain, was standing in the nerve-centre of the most famous police department in the world. The irony was not lost on him as we were introduced to a number of high-ranking and highly decorated officers, in a room with more television screens than a branch of Dixons. This was the NYPD command centre, where every crime and every criminal in the city is tracked and tabbed. Wisely therefore, Adam kept his secret, preferring only to divulge that he 'worked in construction.'

An adjoining room was filled with plush furniture, expensive communications equipment and a plethora of flags and emblems. Dominated by a huge, polished conference table in its centre, and surrounded by wide plasma screens, this could, to an untrained eye like mine, be confused easily with the headquarters of the United Nations or the President's war room. This was the conference room where the biggest meetings in the city took place, and where decisions were made that would shape the future.

Given a moment to think, I tried to picture this room, and the pulse-fingering office next-door, on September 11th. The freshness of Anna's slideshow, coupled with our now close proximity to the Ground Zero that lay behind that perimeter fence, was allowing me to think of nothing else. Yet I couldn't accurately imagine what the experience of that day might have been like here at NYPD command, or even out there on the potholed streets. As an outsider, you couldn't picture what happened that day if you tried, save for playing that news footage around in your head. Somehow it's still all too unreal, too unthinkable, too outrageous. One day, after what is considered a respectful amount of time has elapsed, Hollywood studios will probably be fighting amongst themselves to put out several 'definitive' film versions of that terrible day. But they won't tell you what it was really like, or how it truly impacted New York and its people. The only way to find that out is to walk the streets – to talk to the hoboes, ride in the cabs and eat in the delicatessens. And when you do that, when you see and hear and feel their pain, then you start to get a picture – a perspective even – on what September 11th really meant to this city. All around me crime graphs pointed downwards. Police officers sat idle at their desks. Everyone in this city, the criminals included, had fallen apart.

'Does it make you doubt God,' I asked Val, 'when you see something like September 11th?'

'Do you mean do I blame God?'

'Or does it make you wonder if He even exists?'

'Are you serious?'

'Absolutely.'

'I thought you guys were supposed to be evangelists!'

'I just wondered what you thought. It's all very well for us to talk about suffering and pain, but we haven't felt it in the way that you have. We're outsiders – we didn't lose friends and wives and children and partners. Didn't it make you doubt Him at all?'

Val puffed out his cheeks as we walked down a never-ending corridor.

'I guess as a younger man, maybe I would have got angry with God. But I've seen a lot of things, and I've lived through a lot more than most. I shouldn't even be here, if I tell you the truth. Three years ago I had a car accident – I came off the road and hit a post. I hit it so hard and so fast that my body was thrown right out onto the road through the windshield, and then the car itself came down on top of me. When they found me I must have been in some mess. They took what was left of me down to the hospital, knitted me together with stitches, and pumped a few gallons of blood around my body. They had to remove my spleen and half of my intestines. Now I don't know how anyone could survive an operation like that, let alone the accident, but I did, I'm still here today. And I know that there were people who prayed for me, and I know that my God was with me. So I know what the power of God can do. I've seen how much He loves His children. And when you've seen Him do something like that, right up close, you don't tend to doubt Him.'

Adam and I were both struck by a temporary speechlessness. We drove out of the NYPD car park in silence, and headed down the short road to the biggest crime scene of all.

'You used to be able to see those things,' said Val suddenly after a few minutes, 'wherever you were. Anywhere you were standing in this city, you could just look up and there they were. They were like a reference point – you always knew where you were in the city in relation to those towers.'

'Do you come down here a lot?' I asked, as we pulled in to the workmen's entrance of the site.

'I try not to, truth be told. I haven't been sleeping too well since 9/11. Don't often get much sleep at all.'

Spending too long in a place like Ground Zero would be enough to feed anyone's nightmares. Behind those walls that had shielded my eyes on the previous day, I found a desolate wasteland, a vast building site where the last remains of something big were being cleared. In the centre of the site, a giant mechanical digger poked and nudged at a dusty grey pile of debris. With its huge metal arm, it was prodding away at the last remains of the World Trade Center, of two jet aircraft, and of many long-dead victims. I'd been told that, up to that point, sixteen thousand individual body parts had been recovered from the original dusty grey pile of debris. Around four thousand people had perished on that day, and yet only a few hundred complete bodies had been recovered. The rest of the dead had either been vaporised by the explosion or cut up and scattered throughout the collapse. It sounded like the script of a demonically-inspired horror film, but as the digger continued to rifle through the waste, it became chillingly, vividly real. Beyond the debris, the underground rail station that had once lain hidden was now exposed to the world. To the right of that, the giant metal cross continued to stand defiant, casting a symbolic floodlit shadow in four directions over the uneven ground. Closer to us, a group of workmen shared a coffee and a well-earned rest. Among them, I recognised the man who had approached us on the sidewalk in Queens on the previous afternoon. He looked more relaxed now. Perhaps Tough Talk's prayers had done the trick.

Adam took a moment to catch his breath as I took some photographs. He'd been here before, two years ago, and standing here, on the Ground Zero ground, was more of a shock to him than he'd expected.

'I just can't believe it,' he muttered, to me or to Val or to no one. 'When I stood here before, I looked straight up and those things were so high that you couldn't see the top. I can't believe this. I saw it all on TV, but it's different when you actually stand here. We were going to go up to the top, when we were here. But the queues were too long. And now it's not even here any more.'

Around the vaguely square perimeter of Ground Zero, buildings, shops and restaurants stood empty. Many of them had been built and designed to stand in the shadow of the Twin Towers. Now that the towers were no more, those buildings looked odd and out of place. A crowd mobbing their favourite sports star would look very strange if he suddenly vanished from the midst of them, leaving them all focusing inward on nothing but each other. That was how this felt. Now the mobbing crowd of buildings had nothing to focus in on, save of course for that rusty metal cross.

* * *

An hour later, after unsuccessful attempts in Canal Street and First Avenue, Val finally struck gold. Somewhere in the deepest, darkest corner of Greenwich Village, a man in a pizza parlour told us of his kebab house-owning friend around the corner who served Philly Cheese-steak Sandwiches. We followed the directions, we found the man around the corner. Val ordered three of Baz's finest, with extra pizza sauce, and we sat and devoured. I was not disappointed. Now I could say the same thing about my trip to New York as the rest of the team were saying about theirs. Mission accomplished.

On our way back to the hotel we watched Val prevent a possible rape, as a pack of young, hooded men descended upon a girl walking home on her own. The Sergeant simply wound down the window of the BMW, wished the men a good evening, and watched as they dispersed instantly – each of them evaporating off in a different direction. He waited for a few moments until the girl (who had been completely oblivious to the whole situation) reached a major road, then pulled away. He turned to us, and saw both of our jaws scraping the seats.

'That's 99 per cent of good police work boys,' he said, as if speaking the famous lines of Clint Eastwood or Robert De Niro. 'You've just got to let them know you're there, let them know that you're watching them. And most of the time, thank God, that's all you need to do.'

A terrible crime was averted, and Sgt Suarez drove on. But it was a reminder to all of us that while September 11th had brought even crime in this city to its knees, evil was still alive and well in New York.

'You ever come back to New York, you make sure you call me up,' insisted Val, as he embraced Adam and I outside the Best Western, four hours before we needed to wake up again for our departure. 'You got family here now.' We exchanged e-mail addresses, and even got one of the receptionists from the hotel to take a picture of the three of us. We said fond goodbyes to a man whom we'd only met a few hours ago, and turned a little sadly to go inside. But he called us back and, with a lump in his throat, made a final request.

'Guys, did you get a picture of that cross at Ground Zero.'

'Yes, we took lots of them.'

'Could you send me one please?'

We agreed in an instant. Satisfied, Val got into his BMW and screeched away into the midnight air. And we were left on the sidewalk to contemplate the story we'd unravelled that evening – of the man who'd been caught up in the terror of September 11th, and who'd spent months sleeplessly feeling his way through the aftermath. He didn't understand what had happened, but he refused to blame his God for it. Instead, in looking for hope he still looked heavenward; he still wanted to look towards the cross.

Chapter 10

George, Syd and the Birdman

Less than two weeks after our return trip across the pond, I found myself in the company of Tough Talk once again. This time they had come to my territory, on the London–Surrey borders, to take part in a competition between evangelists. The 'Evangelist Extraordinaire' award – billed as a clash of the soul-saving titans – was to form part of the opening ceremony of the annual national Christian Resources Exhibition, and Tough Talk had been singled out as potential winners. Hence their presence now in Surrey, at the Sandown Racecourse, where this ultimate event in the religious social calendar was being held.

The exhibition itself was much like any other: an Ideal Home or What Car show, but with more vicars and tea. A vast range of stands wound through the main halls of the conference centre, set out in rows and columns – a bizarre combination of a car boot sale and the New York street map. Exhibitors ranged from pew-makers and window-stainers to puppet manufacturers and importers of fair trade coffee. On the corner of one row and another column – the CRE equivalent of 55th and Broadway – stood the Premier Christian Radio stand, and I'd come down, by arranged coincidence, to help man it. A friend and colleague covered for me as I made my way to the 'main arena' (a couple of hundred chairs and a recently-erected stage), where Arthur, Ian, Steve and Marcus had congregated in preparation for their appearance.

The idea of the competition was that each 'act' would get twelve minutes to demonstrate how they use an extraordinary method to assist them in their evangelism. Competing for the title, and a £500 prize, were a comedian/magician, a Welshman who staged mock public executions, a mulleted gentleman known only as 'birdman', and of course, our very own inimitable power-lifters. In a telephone conversation the previous night, Arthur had said something quite profound to me. 'I hope,' he'd said, 'that we come last in this competition. I hope that there are other people who go up there and are absolutely brilliant at communicating the Christian message.' It would be some event, I thought, if that wish was to be granted.

Tough Talk went on first and, in front of a pitiful sprinkling of people, presented an edited-down version of one of the events from Queens or the Bronx, although it was difficult for them to generate the same kind of buzz with an audience of twenty half-awake Brits. When Arthur shouted the words 'Who wants to see some big weights lifted?' the only response came from an old woman in the back row, who yelped with excitement. Tough Talk carried on regardless, determined to make good use of their twelve minutes and at least to wake a few people up.

Over the course of the next ten minutes, things began to improve. Concerned by the loud music that was being played out from the stage, people began to filter out of the main exhibition and into the performance area. A large crowd began to form at the back of the room, at a

safe enough distance to prevent them from having to volunteer for anything. Arthur's testimony caused it's usual
gasps (more of shock than empathy here in Surrey), and
Marcus's lifting somehow managed to get the lifeless
mob cheering. In the front row, one of the judges was
practically out of his seat with excitement. High praise
indeed, considering that this was none other than popular entertainer Syd Little, of Little and Large fame.

Steve took the microphone and ploughed on in a similar vein. All the jokes were flowing freely, and the accent
was in such full swing that even Ian and Arthur began to
have difficulty understanding him. The room was filling
up, and the we're-not-here brigade at the back began to
overflow into some of the rear seats. 'Who are these
men?' whispered what was at last a crowd collectively.

Steve was just at the miracle-healing segment of his
story, when an important looking man with a beard ran
on stage to stop the show. By my watch they'd only had
eight minutes so far – surely there was some mistake.
Steve's mouth remained open for flycatching purposes.

'Excuse me gentlemen' interrupted 'the Beard'.
'Would you mind stopping for a moment? There's someone who'd like to have his photo taken with you.'

He pointed towards the back of the room, and every
pair of eyes followed his arm. There, making his way to
the front of the stage, was the Archbishop of Canterbury
himself, Dr George Carey. Steve's mouth remained open
for flycatching purposes.

'Hello there!' said the Archbishop with trademark
cheerfulness. He looked slightly embarrassed to be walking in mid-performance.

The four big men in the puffa jackets were not expecting this. And though they had no inhibitions when
chatting to drug dealers and life-sentence prisoners, the
appearance of this gentleman in his maroon shirt and

dog collar had stolen the words from their throats. Arthur nodded as he took the clergyman's hand, but wore a strange smile on his face that made him look like he was in pain.

'You know,' said the Archbishop after shaking four twitching hands, 'I used to have a set of weights myself, before the war. But when I returned, my mother had got rid of them!'

'Oh,' quipped Marcus with maximum inappropriateness, 'was that why you decided to change careers?'

A photographer asked everyone on stage to squeeze up together. The picture would go on to appear in *The Times* on the following morning. The four muscular evangelists crowded around the Archbishop as he posed with his elbows resting on the elevated bar. They were pleased to be introduced to an important national figure, and even flattered that he'd asked them to pose with him. But they were not in awe of him. Church politics and networking were not Tough Talk's first concerns after all. But then, that's probably exactly why the Archbishop wanted to have his photo taken with them in the first place.

He went further in his commendation. While the flashbulbs continued to blind him, he took Steve's microphone, leant heavily on the bar and began to pay tribute to the work of Tough Talk in a series of print-friendly soundbites.

'I think it is fantastic,' he said, 'that a group of men like this have found a way to go out into council estates and deprived areas and share stories of how Jesus Christ has changed their lives. Their use of this weightlifting equipment is innovative and shows that Christianity can still be very relevant in British life today. They are a fine example to evangelists everywhere.'

Then, as quickly as he had arrived, the Archbishop promptly disappeared, declining on his way an offer

from Marcus to 'have a go at lifting that'. The Beard indi-
cated that Steve should pick up from where he'd left off,
and incredibly, he managed it. A few more laughs and
gasps were quickly procured from the startled audience,
many of whom had never seen a real live Archbishop
before, and then Ian squeezed in the briefest of gospel
messages. The twelve minutes were up, and Tough Talk
sat down. Syd Little was on his feet in wild applause.

Before the next act, one of the charismatic hosts of the
Evangelist Extraordinaire competition interviewed
the iconic figure whose very presence there had so
excited the crowd. This was clearly a contractually-
agreed opportunity for Syd to plug a Christian cruise, on
which he had been booked to appear as a cabaret artiste.
But having seen the boys perform, Mr Little had other
issues on his mind.

'I've got to say I've never seen anything like that,'
gushed Syd, in response to a question about his cruise. 'It
was loud, it was slick, it was exciting. I've got to say that as
a performer myself, that would be one hard act to follow.'

This must have made the magician, whose turn it was
to take the platform next, feel really good about his
chances, especially considering that Syd had been introduced as one of the judges. Nevertheless he performed
well. He was articulate, he cracked a couple of big-laugh-
producing jokes (these involved self-deprecation and
toilet humour – favourites with Christians), and he wore
a very loud shirt. Ultimately though, he was a cabaret
man, much like Syd, and following a group of noise-
makers like Tough Talk proved to be too much of an
uphill struggle. Also, his main magic trick revolved
around a balloon, and he only had one balloon, and it
had a hole in it, and nobody had any spares, so his big
moment fell a bit flat.

The magician was followed by the public executioner: a man with a giant wooden guillotine and one of those microphone headsets that Jan-Michael Vincent used to wear in *Airwolf*. The idea of his routine was that he asked a volunteer to impersonate a member of the French aristocracy by placing their head on the chopping block, while he talked to a then-captivated audience about God. As he built up to the rather inevitable conclusion of his act, he used the guillotine as a metaphor for the cross on which Jesus had died. It was a powerful image, which brought home the story of Jesus' death and sacrifice with real poignancy. And while the Guillotine is no longer used in modern-day society as a means for disposing of heretics, it is likely that a mocked up electric chair may have lacked something in the visual suspense department. Thus, at the end of the executioner's presentation, the blade fell, the crowd gasped, and the volunteer escaped death thanks to the fact that it was only an illusion. Which was disappointing, from a spectator's point of view.

The final act shall be described, but no judgement shall be passed. The 'birdman' was a northern minister whose evangelistic exploits were so renowned that once they had even landed him a sofa spot on ITV's flagship *This Morning with Richard and Judy* programme. The hosts' introduction gave us no more information than that, but when a small, unlikely-looking man took to the stage, with a laptop under his arm and no wings on his back, I became very inquisitive. At the back of the room, a large batch of people tiptoed back towards the main exhibition hall.

The remaining audience watched as the man commentated on some home video footage. On a large white screen positioned above the stage, a man with a James

Bond-esque jetpack was flying over a British council estate, shouting from a megaphone and dragging behind him a wide yellow parachute that bore the word REPENT! in thick black letters. In many ways he looked like an airborne version of the classic sandwich-board-wearing street preacher. He sailed past tower blocks and over communal gardens, belting out his evangelistic message as he went. But something went wrong – this jetpack was not as reliable as Bond's – and the man, the machine and the giant wind-filled banana came crashing down to earth.

'Birdman' then explained that the man in the film was none other than himself, and that he had shown us the footage to demonstrate how he had taken the message of Jesus Christ into a rough council estate. (He did not reveal whether or not he'd used the airborne megaphone approach to try to impersonate the voice of God.) Then, he showed unconnected footage of himself shouting abuse at Monica Lewinsky during a book signing, where he told her to repent too.

As I said, I'll let you draw your own conclusions.

Somehow, despite the level of competition, Tough Talk had done enough to be announced as the '2002 Evangelists Extraordinaire'. Most of the boys had already headed back to their places of work, so Arthur proudly accepted the cheque. 'We'll be able to buy a few hundred Bibles with this,' he said, and received a warm round of applause from the crowd. He also picked up a nice certificate, which went in Jacqui's handbag.

Arthur loaded up the van amid autograph requests from pensioners and networking attempts from would-be Christian media tycoons. I knew that this would be the last time I'd see him for a while, so I pushed myself through the crowd and took hold of his bulky shoulders with both hands.

'Thanks,' I said. 'Thanks for everything over the last few weeks. I've had the time of my life.'

'That's alright son,' he replied, genuine as ever. 'It's been good to have you with us.'

I was suddenly filled with sadness. I'd enjoyed this madcap six months so much, and now it was at an end. Now it was time to return to the world of Christian journalism – of cat-up-a-vicarage-tree stories and flying preachers. Stories like Tough Talk's don't come along every day of the week.

'Of course,' said Arthur, 'you could always come with us now. We're off to Slovakia on a quick mission – there's space in the van if you're interested.'

I declined politely – fourteen hours in that van had been quite enough for one lifetime – and said a final goodbye. Slowly, Arthur lumbered out of view, off to plough new mission fields and lift more weights. I'd miss him.

* * *

It's hard for me to know who you might be, reading this book. But I believe that, whoever you are, there is something in the story of Tough Talk which demands your consideration.

If you're a Christian, who picked this up after being informed that it was a pleasant piece of coffee-table puff, then apologies (unless you do think it's coffee-table puff, in which case, no apology needed). Tough Talk are, according to Syd Little and his distinguished panel of judges, one of the most dynamic and ground-breaking evangelistic groups at work in the United Kingdom today. They've found a way of communicating the gospel to people like themselves – people with dark backgrounds, criminals, addicts and purveyors of violence. They use powerlifting as a means of connecting with these kinds of people, and then they use honest, real storytelling to get their message across. And as a strange kind of by-product – much in the same way that people making soap find that the floor gets covered in that stuff they used to market as 'Silly Ooze' or 'Ectoplasm' – they also reach schoolchildren who've never been in trouble, housewives who'd never consider infidelity, and men like me who think gym is a four-letter word. But they can't reach everyone. If the dwindling British church is to have a fighting chance it needs more than a handful of decent salesmen. Perhaps that's where you come in.

Arthur often makes the comment on stage that Tough Talk only lift weights when they speak because that's what they do even when they are not evangelising. 'If we were singers or dancers, we'd sing or dance for you,' he'd say. 'But we're not. We're powerlifters and body-builders, and so we lift weights for you.' It may seem an obvious point, but there is actually a powerful evangelistic model there.

Some people would be completely turned off if they witnessed a Tough Talk meeting. But that does not necessarily mean that they are resistant to the gospel – it probably just means that they have little time for meat-heads pumping iron. If Tough Talk had been a group of footballers, or ballet dancers, or musicians, or beauticians, or golfers, or filmmakers, perhaps those people would not be turned off.

It seems to me that the Tough Talk model could be adopted and manipulated by any number of evangelistic groups in any number of ways. All that is needed are two key elements: an attention-grabbing, interest-involving attraction, and down-to-earth, relevant, honest storytelling. If the church considered such a model when approaching cold-sell evangelism, perhaps the manic street preacher in the sandwich board – airborne or otherwise – would become a thing of the past.

If you're a man living in the age when Schwarzenegger is still king, then I can recommend few better role models than the gentlemen who formed the subject of this story. First and foremost, they love their wives and families, not themselves. Ian and Arthur were fortunate enough to be able to bring their families with them to New York, and Steve was practically torn apart over the few days he spent there because he missed his wife and children so much. You can't counterfeit the emotions that I witnessed in all those people as I tried to learn their stories – their families are built on love, and there is no better foundation.

The Tough Talkers are also far more than the sum of their muscles. They are muscle-bound mainly due to the lives that they once led, but they are all still incredibly strong men. And every time I watched that strength channelled, it was in a positive or harmless direction. They are not fighters. Steve, whose bloody knuckles barely had a chance to heal over twenty years, has not been involved in a single act of violence since he became a Christian.

Besides love and pacifism, they also display a number of qualities conducive to what the Bible would call a real man. They are honest men. They are honourable men. They don't get drunk, they don't swear, they don't take drugs. But they do provide strong leadership in their respective households, and they do listen to their wives and children. And yet with all these apparent restrictions and abstinences placed on their lives, they still manage to live as real men in the real world. They still go to the pub, the gym, and the football ground. They still keep their eyes open, and their ears to the ground, and make sure they know what's going on around them. And they still manage, at all times, to have a laugh. It's not only a positive act to follow; it's also rewarding and enjoyable.

But in all these men do, at work, rest and play, they're only trying to emulate a man who lived by very similar virtues and played by very similar rules – Jesus Christ Himself.

If you're not a Christian, then I hope that the stories of Arthur, Ian and Steve have caused you to stop and think. The biggest problem with modern Christianity is that it continues to do its best to appear entirely irrelevant to the rest of society. That's why the J-word has been rendered meaningless in our culture, where once it referred to the greatest revolutionary in the history of the world. That's why when we ask God to 'Save the Queen' or 'Bless America', we're no longer serious. And with a fragmented church, divided up into Catholics, Anglicans, Methodists, Baptists and so on, it's hardly likely that things will change very much. But Arthur, Ian and Steve aren't concerned with that sort of thing. They were rescued from the brink of destruction when they personally encountered God Himself – a God who refuses to be put in a box, or tied to a denomination, and who probably doesn't care about what kind of words are used to worship Him, or how much water his followers are dunked in.

Despite the world's best attempts to engineer otherwise, Christianity is not a complicated faith and, on one level at least, God is not a complicated God. The message of Jesus – a real person who really died on the cross, and really rose again – was simply that the people of the world should follow Him, and have a relationship with

Him. That's about it. A lot of the other stuff was just tagged on by clergymen with time on their hands.

I believe that the members of Tough Talk prove that Christianity is relevant today. I've been privileged enough to watch the proof unfold from a first-hand position. They were unashamed of that simple message when they became the first people to tell it to Châtel in France, and they were unashamed of it as they walked into the New York ghettos and told it to some of the most hardened men and women in the Western world. They'd tell the same message to you in a pub in London, or on a street in Glasgow, or in a prison in Texas. And whether you chose to believe that message or not, you'd probably be forced to concede that the Christian faith might still have something to say to today's culture.

So if, through reading this, you feel inspired to investigate Christianity further, I can make only one recommendation to you. Pick up a Bible, turn three quarters of the way through to the gospel of Mark, and read about the real man behind the J-word. Tough Talk only exists to ask people like you to do that, and to make your own mind up about God. They don't want to patronise, to preach or teach at you. They want to tell you their stories, and then ask you to think about what they mean. That's what this book has attempted to do too. So over to you.

And finally, if you're Bob Spzalek, Syd Little, the Birdman, the Archbishop of Canterbury, Anna, Val, French, American, Little Phil, Baz, Andy Hawthorne, Zola, Julia Fisher or either of the bearded people referred to in this story and you happen to be reading, apologies for any offence caused. I only told it like I saw it, and it was only one perspective.

A comment from The Most Revd & Rt Hon George Carey, former Archbishop of Canterbury

'I think it is fantastic that a group of men like this have found a way to go out into council estates and deprived areas and share stories of how Jesus Christ has changed their lives. Their use of this weightlifting equipment is innovative and shows that Christianity can still be very relevant in British life today. They are a fine example to evangelists everywhere.'

For further information on Tough Talk contact:

Tough Talk
119 George Lane
South Woodford
London
E18 1AN

Tel/Fax 020 8923 6190

Email:arthurwhite@talk21.com
www.toughtalk.org.uk

Registered Charity No 1084886

C.W.E.S.T.

Christians Who Evangelise, Serve and Train co-hosted
the 'Evangelist Extraordinaire' event with ship-of-
fools.com. C.W.E.S.T.'s members include stars from
theatre, pop music and film

Contact Steve Lyn Evans, evanscwest@aol.com
or 07764 60 70 60

Tough Talk

Arthur White, Steve Johnson and Ian McDowall, with Millie Murray

The stories of Arthur White, Steve Johnson and Ian McDowall, their lives changed by the grace of God.

From drugs, alcohol, violence and immoral relationships they have been able, not only to overcome and endure the harshness of their lives, but to dedicate their time to telling people that they do not have to remain in that state; that the hope that these men have is available to everyone, no matter what their background or lifestyle.

ISBN: 1-86024-378-9

Paperback £6.99

Tough Talk New Testament

New Century Version

Pocket-sized paperback New Testaments in a modern translation, which include preliminary pages written by members of Tough Talk. Two cover options are available: one with photos and one without.

With photos
ISBN: 0-86024-277-4

Without photos
ISBN: 0-86024-278-2

Paperback £4.99

Tough Talk (video)

You would think it was fictional, but these are true stories of night club bouncers, minders and debt collectors. Watch and listen as they tell their stories of how their lives have been powerfully changed.

Dave Golds was a bodyguard for the Turkish Mafia and Colombian drug cartel. We travel to Spain with Dave and hear how he pursued a man who had disappeared with over £1 million across Europe in cash and drugs.

Steve Johnson was a bouncer in several East London pubs. Hard as they come, he was so drunk one night that he didn't even fell the broken glass thrust into his face after he had offended a customer.

World Champion powerlifter **Arthur White** takes us back to his debt collecting days, when he would regularly carry a diver's knife tied to his wrist to persuade people to pay up.

These stories will shock and challenge you. How can these men have changed from such an evil way of life?

ISBN: 1-86024-344-4 – Video £9.99

Tough Talk in New York (video)

This second video gives the best insight so far, into what the Tough Talk team do now, as we follow them on tour in some of the roughest suburbs of New York.

See how Tough Talk use their incredible strength and weightlifting abilities to draw a crowd, and then proclaim, unashamedly, the Gospel message. Watch them as they penetrate some of the hardest young offenders' institutions in the USA bringing the love of Christ to those who have been written-off by all around them.

This fast moving and insightful video will inspire churches towards creative evangelism, demonstrating how lives can be transformed through the proclamation of the Gospel message.

ISBN: 1-86024-224-3 – Video £9.99